HOW TO PLAY BASS GUITAR.

Arnie Berle.

Amsco Publications
New York/London/Sydney/Cologne

US International Standard Book Number: 0.8256.2397.9
UK International Standard Book Number: 0.7119.0451.0

Exclusive Distributors:
Music Sales Corporation
225 Park Avenue South, New York, NY 10003 USA
Music Sales Limited
8/9 Frith Street, London W1V 5TZ England
Music Sales Pty. Limited
120 Rothschild Street, Rosebery, Sydney, NSW 2018, Australia

Printed in the United States of America by
Vicks Lithograph and Printing Corporation

Contents

To the Teacher

In this book I have tried to provide a source for bass teachers that is understandable, yet progressive; one that fills a gap in the body of published teaching material currently available. Here you will find the outline for a method that progresses logically and gives the student the basic reading, theoretical, and technical skills that will enable him to create a solid and interesting bass line without ignoring the necessities of good musicianship.

I have included scales, chord progressions, and studies that take the beginning bass player up the neck, so that he will be familiar with most closed as well as open positions. All of the information is supported by musical examples, while leaving room for the teacher to add additional supplementary material in the form of more studies, text, or even appropriate standards. The *Solo Book for Bass Guitar* (Acorn Music Press) can be used in places where the teacher does not have additional material handy, or as another source to encourage advanced technique for the beginner in reading as well as playing.

To the Student

A good bass player is one of the most sought after musicians by any kind of band. Whether you want to be the foundation—a "musician's musician"—or whether you want to be up front with your musicality and presence like a Stanley Clarke, Jaco Pastorius, or Paul McCartney, you will always be the musical backbone for the group. You have probably seen a bad band pull off a performance simply because the bass player was good. When you have finished working through *How to Play Bass Guitar,* I hope that you will understand just how important a good bass player can be and how you can be that bass player.

With this book, and a good teacher, you will learn all the basic theory, scales, chord progressions, and technique that you will need to build good, solid bass lines. After you have finished, it is up to you where you want to go musically: Jazz, fusion, rock riffs and solos will all be easily within your reach when you have mastered the skills in *How to Play Bass Guitar.*

Getting Started

Right-Hand Technique

Fingerstyle

Playing with the fingers is the standard way of playing acoustic bass, and that tradition has been carried over to the electric bass by most musicians. Keep the right hand and wrist relaxed with the fingers slightly curved. The thumb should rest approximately half an inch above the E (lowest) string. The first or second finger is used to strike the string and follows through until it comes to rest on the next string (a rest stroke). When you are playing the E string, the finger should finish in the air, as if there were an imaginary fifth string.

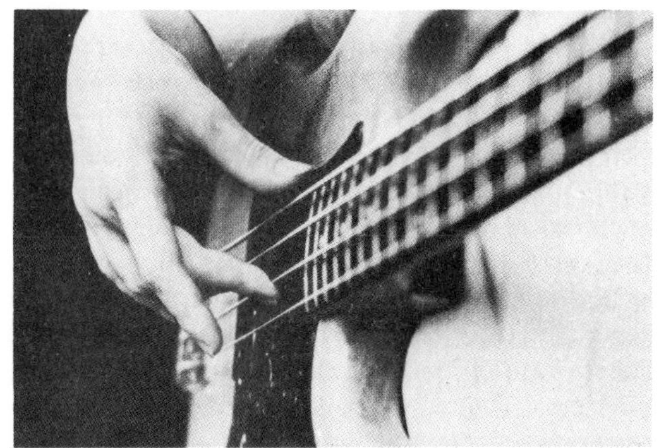

Proper completion of a rest stroke.

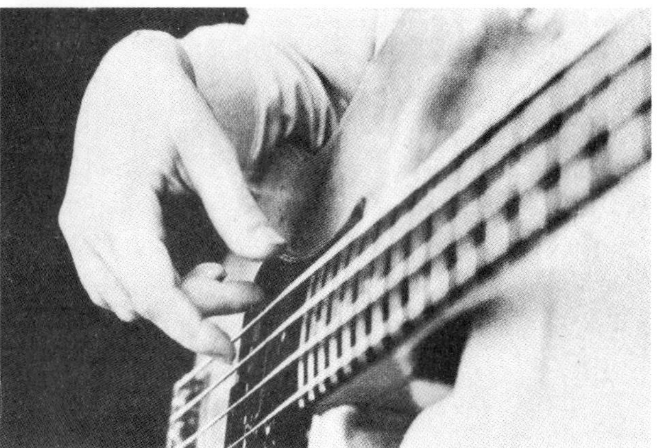

Correct hand and finger position after striking the E string.

Pickstyle

Although most electric bass players prefer to use their fingers, a number of excellent bassists play with a pick. Don't hold the pick stiffly, but rather rest it on the joint of the first finger and use your thumb to give the slightest resistance. Use the photograph below as a guide.

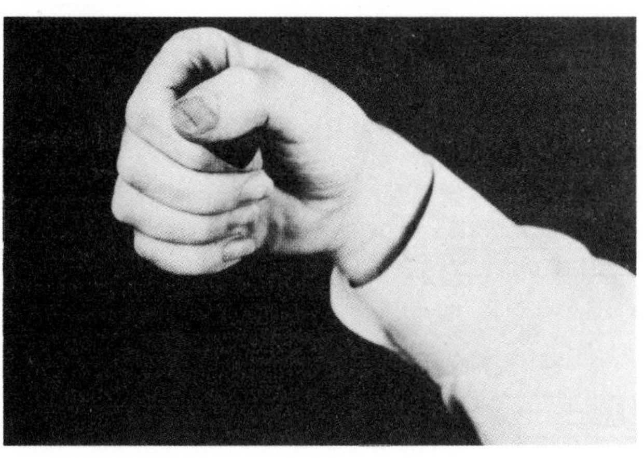

Basic Left-Hand Technique

Ideally, each finger should press the string at the fret that it is nearest: the index finger pressing down at the first fret, the second finger at the second, and so on. However, the distance between frets is much wider at the top of the neck, and decreases as you move closer to the body of the instrument. If at first you have difficulty playing, for example, the third fret with the third finger, it is acceptable to use the fourth finger, and simply change position for the fourth fret.

Press down securely and aim for a clear tone without buzzes.

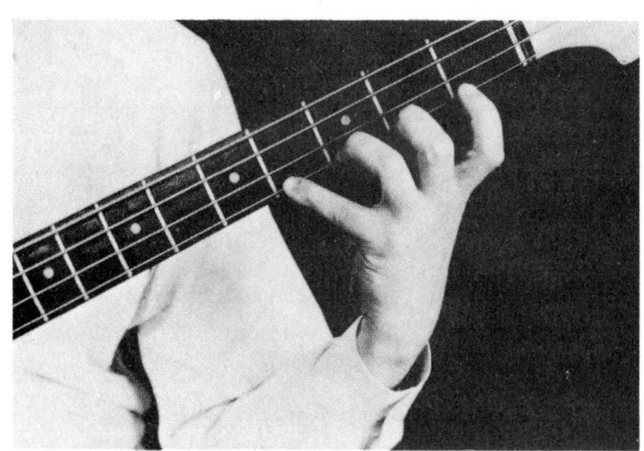

Basic Music Theory

Music is written on a *staff* which is made up of five lines and four spaces.

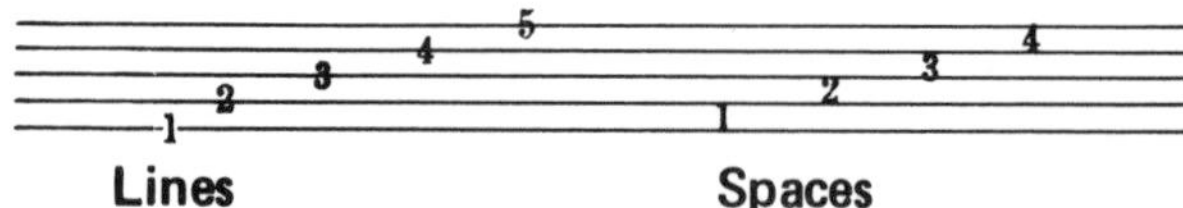

The *bass* or *F clef* is placed at the beginning of each staff. The dots above and below the second line tell where the note *F* is located. All the other notes in this clef take their location from this F.

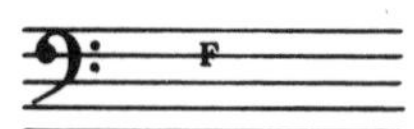

The example below gives the letter name for each line in the bass clef.

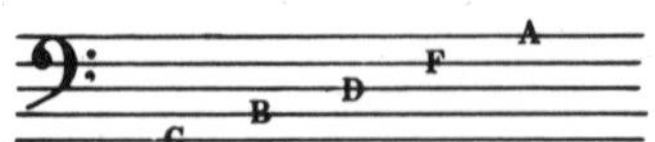

The spaces are named as follows:

Notice that the musical alphabet consists of only seven letters. Below are the letter names for all the lines and spaces in the bass clef. After the letter G the musical alphabet returns to the letter A and keeps on repeating itself.

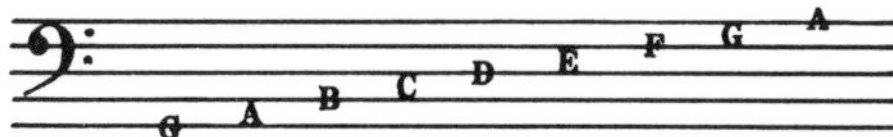

Notes are symbols placed on the staff that represent different *pitches* (high or low sounds). The higher the note is placed on the staff, the higher the pitch; the lower it is on the staff, the lower the pitch. Notes take their names from the line or space on which they are placed.

Notes written on or between *ledger lines* represent pitches that cannot be included within the staff.

Music is divided into *measures* by vertical lines called *barlines.*

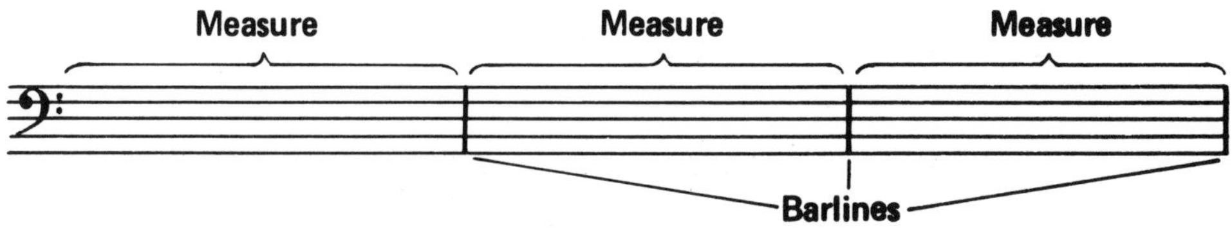

A *time signature* is placed at the beginning of a piece of music to indicate how the measures are to be counted. Taking $\frac{4}{4}$ or *common time* (**C**) as an example, it is explained as follows:

The top number indicates the number of beats or counts in each measure—in this case, four.

The bottom number indicates which kind of note gets one beat. When four is the bottom number, a quarter note receives one beat.

Repeat signs consist of double dots and double barlines and indicate the repetition of a certain section of music.

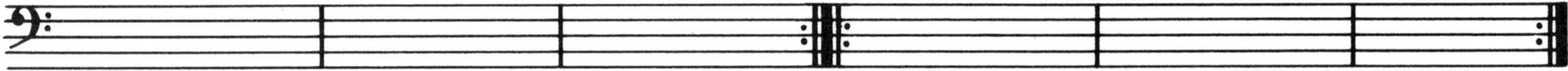

Repeat from the beginning. *Repeat everything between the signs.*

You may have already noticed that notes can be written in different ways. These variations in notation together with the time signature indicate how many beats a note should be held. When the bottom number in a time signature is four, as in $\frac{2}{4}$, $\frac{3}{4}$, and $\frac{4}{4}$, the following time values are observed:

For every note there is a *rest* sign with the same number of beats.

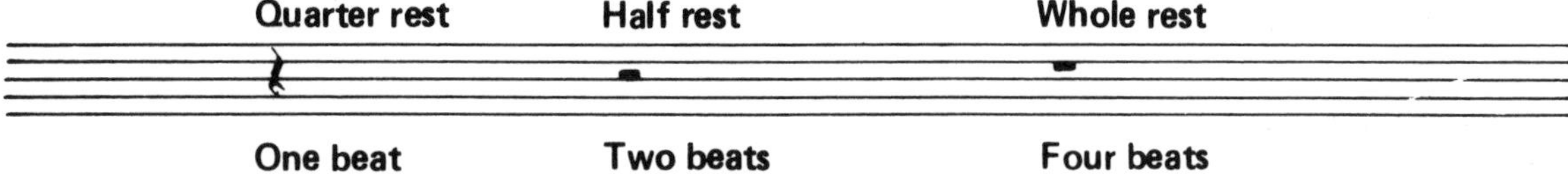

Open-String Studies

The following diagram shows the names of the notes that are produced by the *open* (unfretted) strings.

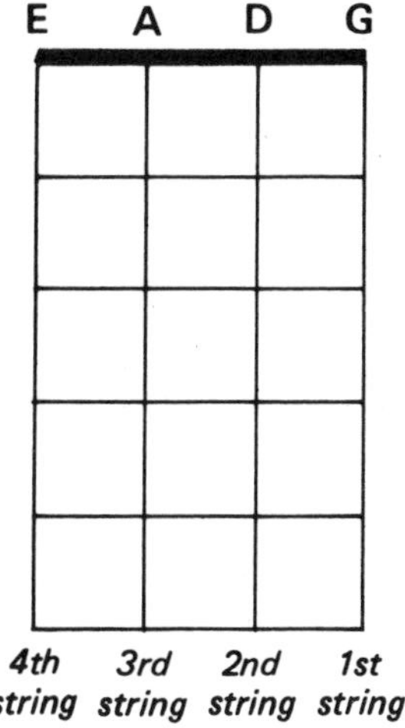

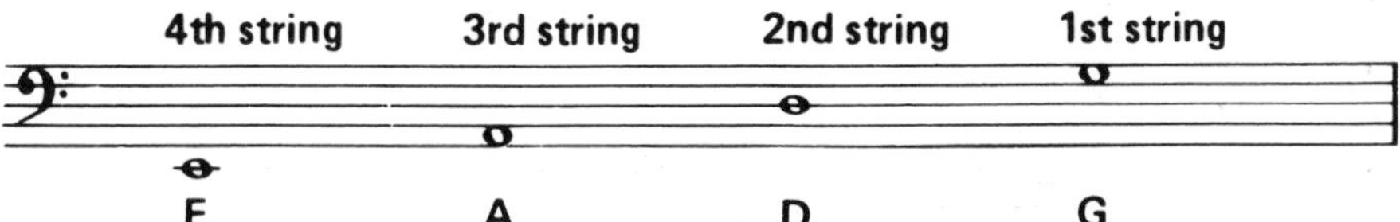

Whole Notes

A whole note, as you may recall, is held for four counts. Play the following exercise based on the open strings using whole notes. Be sure to count aloud and tap your foot four times for each note.

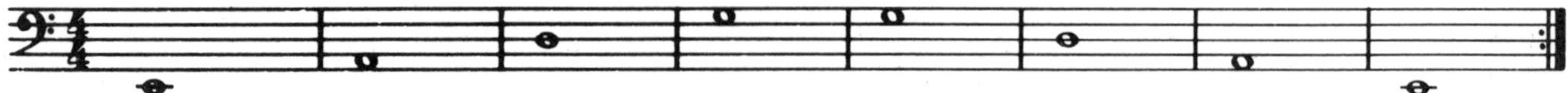

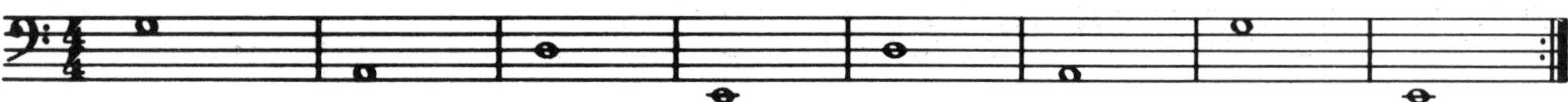

Half Notes

Half notes are held for two counts. Continue to count aloud, tap your foot, and play slowly and smoothly.

Combining Whole Notes and Half Notes

Count: 1 2 3 4 1 2 3 4 etc.

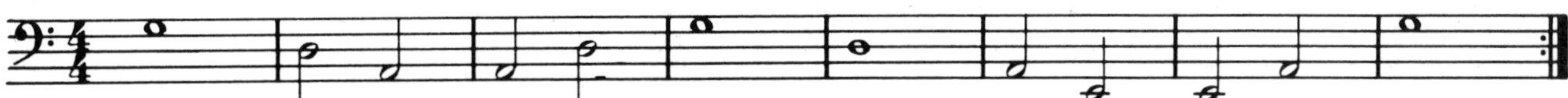

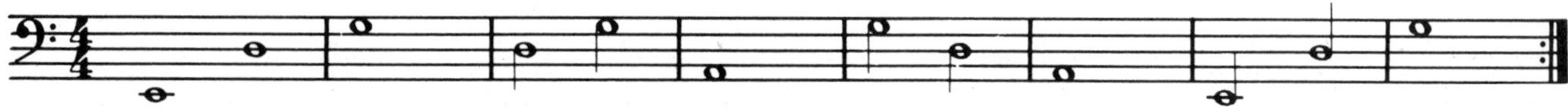

Quarter Notes

A quarter note is held for one count. The following exercises are based on combinations of quarter, half, and whole notes.

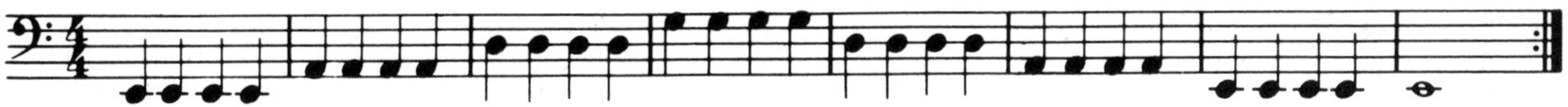

Count: 1 2 3 4 1 2 3 4 etc.

Count: 1 2 3 4 1 2 3 4 etc.

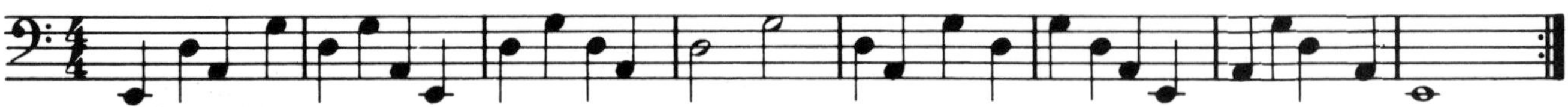

Count: 1 2 3 4 1 2 3 4 etc.

Dotted Half Notes

A dotted half note is held for three counts.

Count: 1 2 3 1 2 3 etc.

Count: 1 2 3 1 2 3 etc.

Playing Notes on the Fingerboard

Notes on the Fourth String

Before playing notes on the fingerboard it is important that you understand the meaning of the words *sharp* and *flat.* A sharp (♯) *raises* a note a *half step.* A flat *lowers* a note a half step.

Notes that are played on the same fret and string, but have two different names are called *enharmonic.* For example, F♯ and G♭ are both played on the fourth string at the second fret.

Figure 1 shows the names of the notes on the fourth string using sharps; Figure 2 shows the names of the notes on the fourth string using flats.

Play the following exercises very slowly and continue to count aloud.

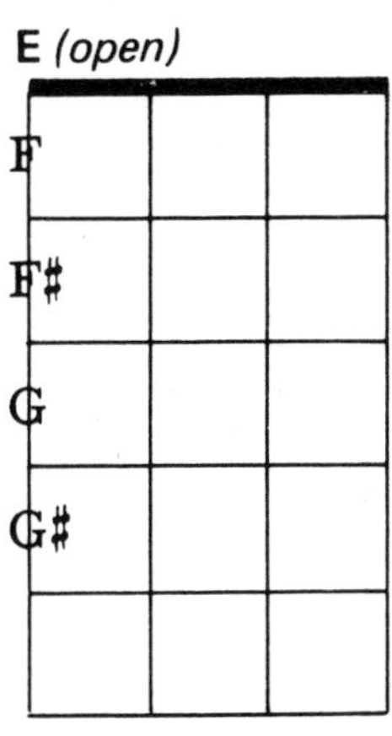

Figure 1

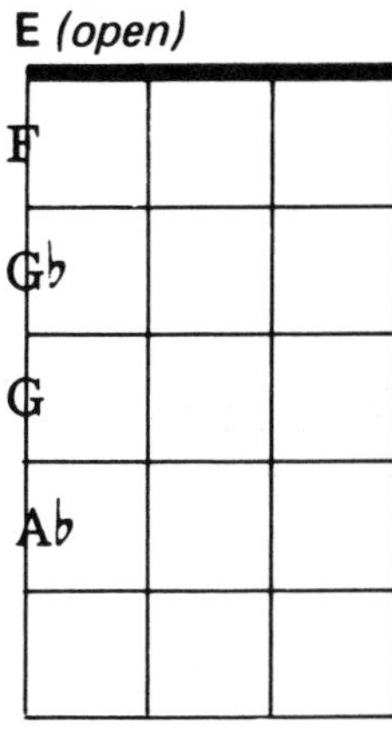

Figure 2

The change in pitch indicated by a sharp or a flat lasts for a measure, unless the note is preceded by a *natural* (♮).

A natural cancels out a sharp or flat, restoring a note to its "natural" pitch.

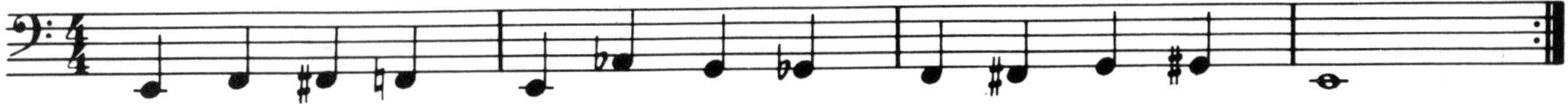

Notes on the Third String

Figure 3 shows the notes on the third string using sharps; Figure 4 shows the notes on the third string using flats.

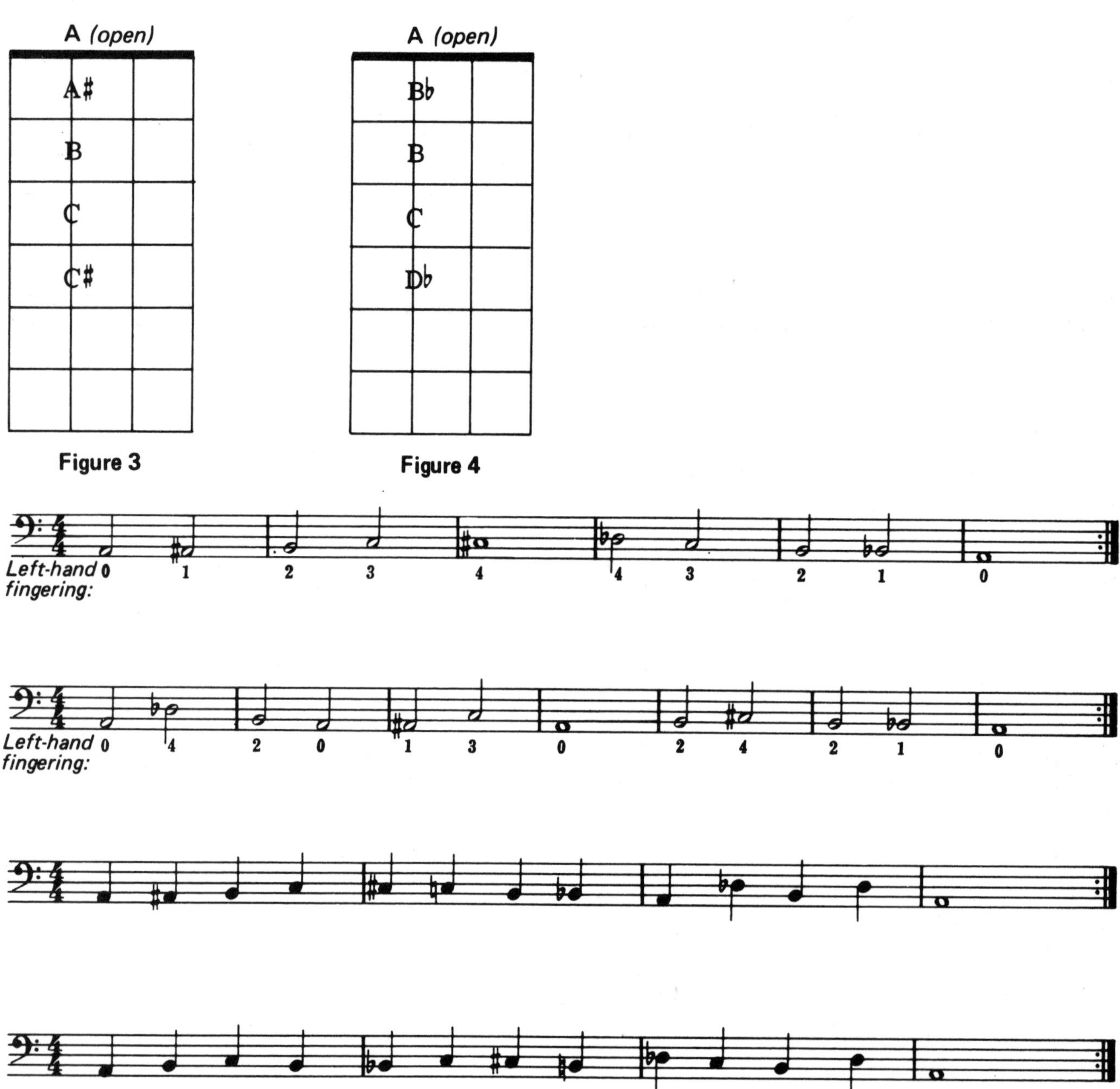

The following exercises combine notes on the fourth and third strings.

Notes on the Second String

Figure 5 shows the notes on the second string using sharps; Figure 6 shows them using flats.

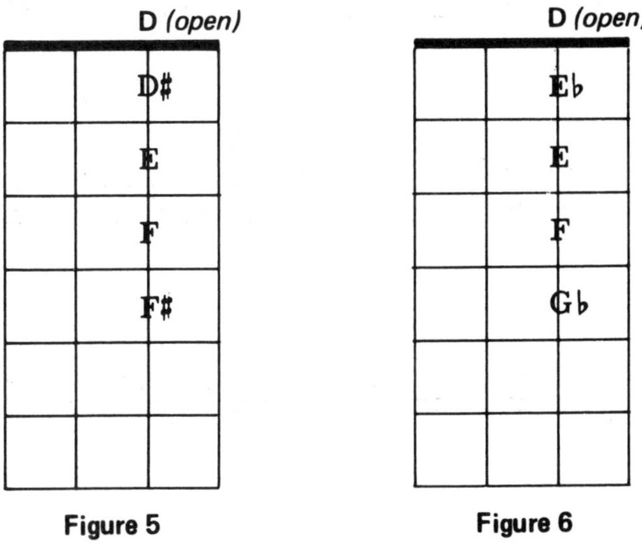

Figure 5

Figure 6

These exercises combine notes on the fourth, third, and second strings.

Notes on the First String

Figure 7 shows the notes on the first string using sharps; Figure 8 shows the notes on the first string using flats.

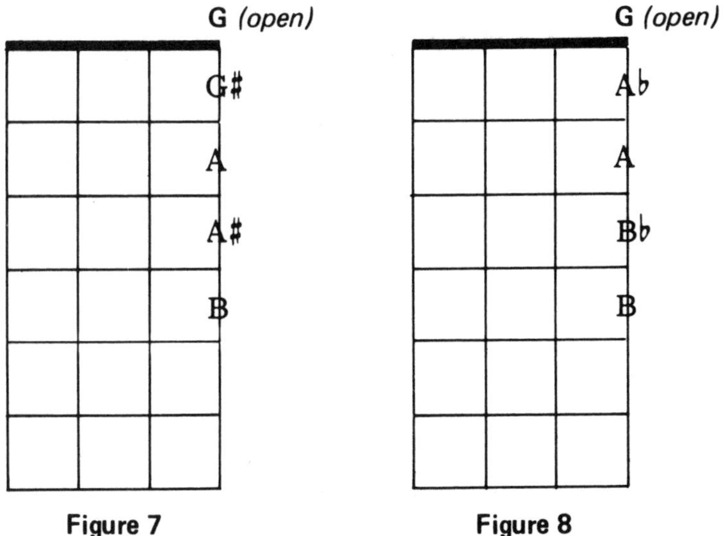

Figure 7

Figure 8

These exercises combine notes on all four strings.

Keys and Major Scales

A *key* is a group of tones or pitches all related to one common tone.
Below is a melody using the tones from the key of C Major. All of these tones have a definite relationship to the C, which we call the *tonic* or *key note.*

A *scale* is made up of the notes of a key placed in alphabetical order. Below is a C Major scale.

C Major Scale

Constructing the Major Scale

A *major scale* is a succession of *whole steps* (two frets) and *half steps* (one fret). The half step occurs naturally between the third and fourth notes and between the seventh and eighth notes. All other notes are a whole step apart. Play through the C Major scale below, paying close attention to where the whole and half steps occur.

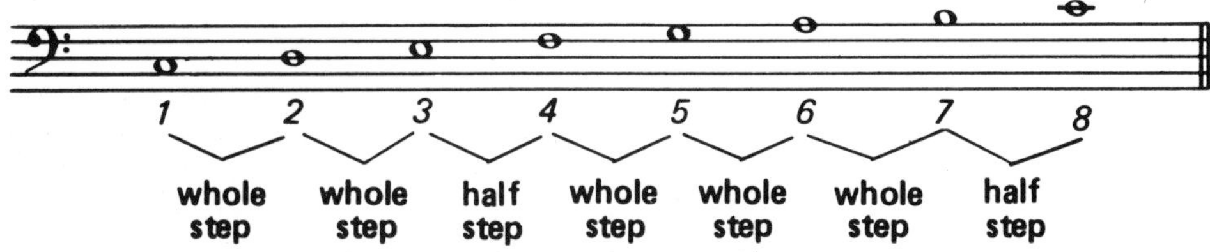

Since the last note in the scale written above is one half step above B, it is played on the next fret: fifth fret, first string.

G Major Scale: Notice in the example of the G Major scale below, that the F has been sharped in order to maintain the correct relationship of whole and half steps.

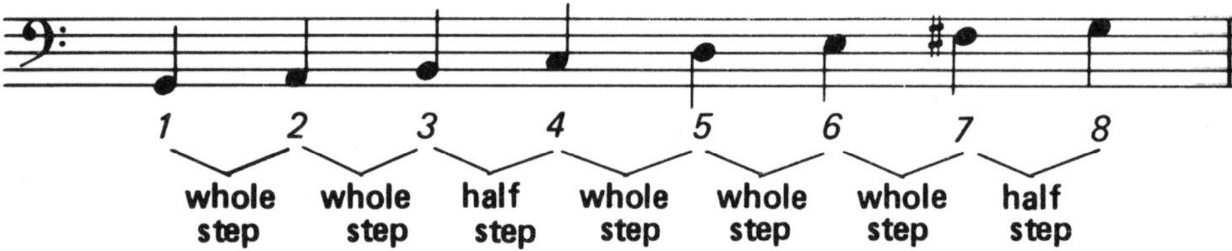

F Major Scale: In the F Major scale below, the B has been flatted so that there will be a half step between the third and fourth notes, and a whole step between the fourth and fifth notes.

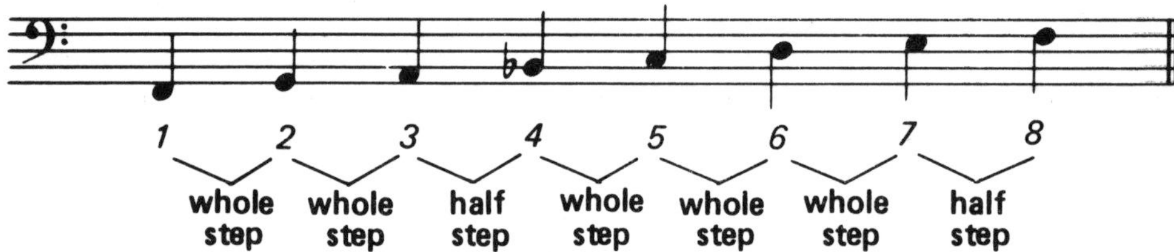

Key Signature

A *key signature* is the group of sharps or flats at the beginning of a piece of music and indicates not only what notes are to be consistently sharped or flatted, but also what key the piece is written in. Below are the key signatures for the scales given above.

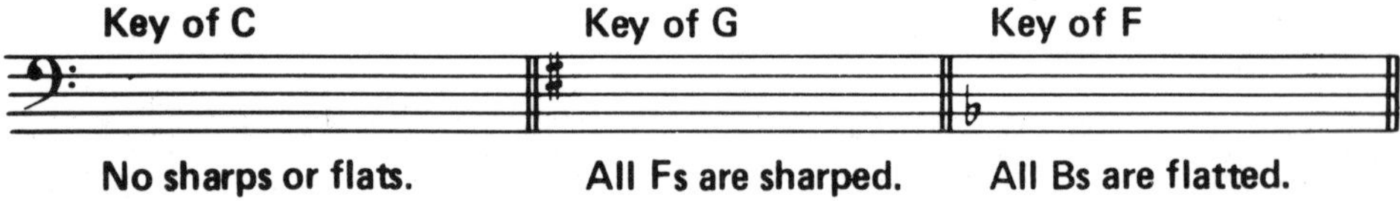

Accidentals

A sharp or a flat next to a note and not found in the key signature is called an *accidental.* In the example below, F♯ is the accidental.

Intervals

An *interval* is the distance between two notes, and is based on the same whole and half step relationships that occur in a major scale. Below is an example of the intervals contained in the major scale.

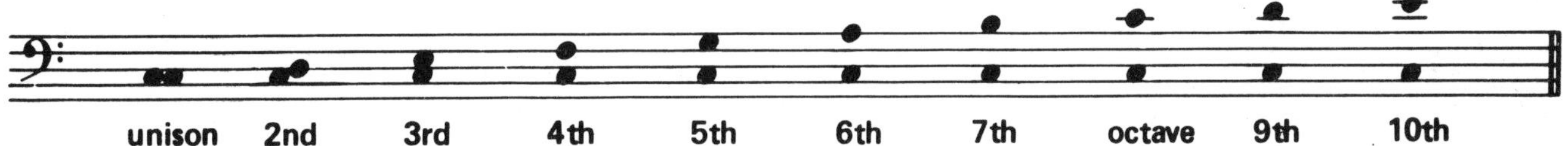

Studies in Three Keys

The following studies are designed to help you read music in three keys: C, G, and F. Be sure to count all note values correctly.

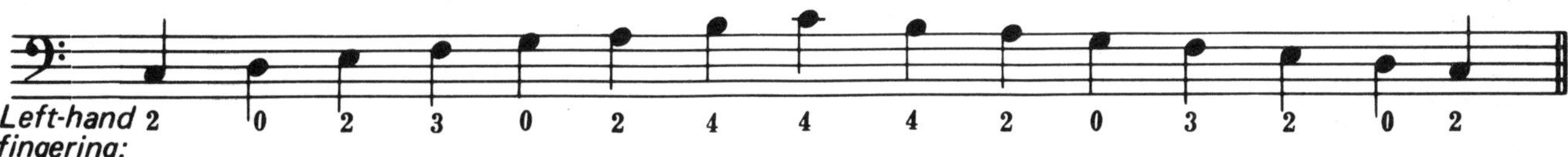

Key of G (contains F♯)

Key of F (contains B♭)

Eighth Notes

Quarter notes may be divided into *eighth notes.* In $\frac{4}{4}$ time, two eighth notes would be equal to one quarter note, and one eighth note would be counted as one-half of a beat.
Eighth notes can be written two different ways: with either a *flag* (for single eighth notes) or a *beam* (for two or more eighth notes).

To count eighth notes, begin by counting quarter notes. Once you have established an even, steady rhythm, "fill in" the space between each count with an "end." Try mixing eighth notes and quarter notes.

An *eighth rest* (𝄾) can come on the upbeat .

It can also occur on the downbeat.

In the following exercise be sure not to rush the upbeat rests.

In this next exercise all the eighth rests come on the downbeats.

This exercise combines eighth rests on downbeats and upbeats.

Studies in B-Flat and D

The following studies are designed to help you develop fluency in the keys of B♭ and D.

Key of B♭ (contains B♭ and E♭)

Key of D (contains F♯ and C♯)

Chords

For the bass player, studying chords as well as scales is one of the most important parts of his musical education. A bass player must be able to create a bass line from any given series of chords. The bass line should outline the essence of the song being played so that a soloist can follow the chord changes in a tune by listening to the bass player.

Major Chords

Chords are formed from the notes of a scale. By taking the first, third and fifth notes of the major scale we form the major chord.

The first note of the scale (the tonic) is called the *root* of the chord, the third note of the scale the third of the chord, and the fifth note of the scale the fifth of the chord. The notes of the chord may be played in any order.

C Major Chord with Variations

Forming the G Major Chord

Forming the F Major Chord

Doubling Chord Tones

When playing four beats to a measure, you may double one of the chord tones (play it twice).

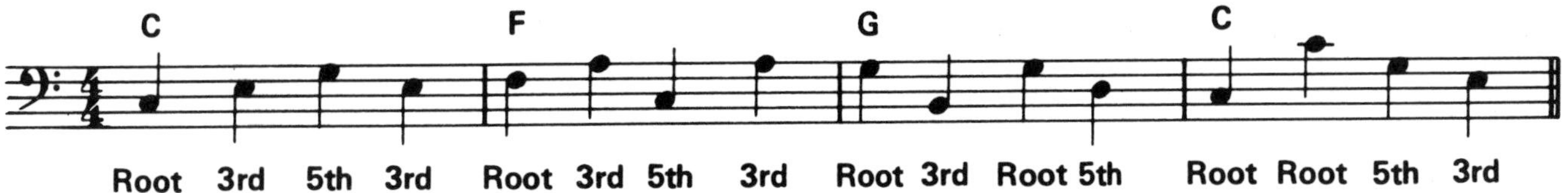

Chord Types

There are four basic chord types: major, minor, augmented, and diminished. By knowing the formula for each chord type, you can build any chord you need. The table below lists the formula for each chord type; it is based on the major scale. For example, to build a C Diminished chord, take the first note, the flatted third note, and the flatted fifth note of the C Major scale, and that will give you the C Diminished chord, C-E♭ -G♭ .

Chord Type	Symbol	Formula	Example
Major	*letter-name*	1 3 5	C
Minor	m *or* –	1♭3 5	Cm *or* C–
Augmented	Aug *or* +	1 3♯5	C Aug *or* C+
Diminished	Dim *or* °	1♭3♭5	C Dim *or* C°

The following table lists the notes of all of the four basic chord types. In some cases the enharmonic equivalent of a particular note is used to avoid a double-sharp or a double-flat—B Aug, for example.

CHORD	MAJOR	MINOR	AUGMENTED	DIMINISHED
C	C E G	C Eb G	C E G#	C Eb Gb
Db	Db F Ab	Db Fb Ab	Db F A	Db Fb Abb (Db E G)
D	D F# A	D F A	D F# A#	D F Ab
Eb	Eb G Bb	Eb Gb Bb	Eb G B	Eb Gb Bbb (Eb Gb A)
E	E G# B	E G B	E G# B#	E G Bb
F	F A C	F Ab C	F A C#	F Ab Cb
Gb	Gb Bb Db	Gb Bbb Db	Gb Bb D	Gb Bbb Dbb (Gb A C)
G	G B D	G Bb D	G B D#	G Bb Db
Ab	Ab C Eb	Ab Cb Eb	Ab C E	Ab Cb Ebb (Ab B D)
A	A C# E	A C E	A C# E#	A C Eb
Bb	Bb D F	Bb Db F	Bb D F#	Bb Db Fb
B	B D# F#	B D F#	B D# G	B D F

Chord Studies

The following exercises will take you through the four basic chord types. It is important that you memorize the fingerings and the sound of each chord type. Notice that sometimes the D♭ and G♭ chords are used and at other times the C♯ and F♯ chords are used. This is done simply to avoid the use of the double-sharp or double-flat wherever possible. The third of each chord is doubled to strengthen the sound.

Major Chords

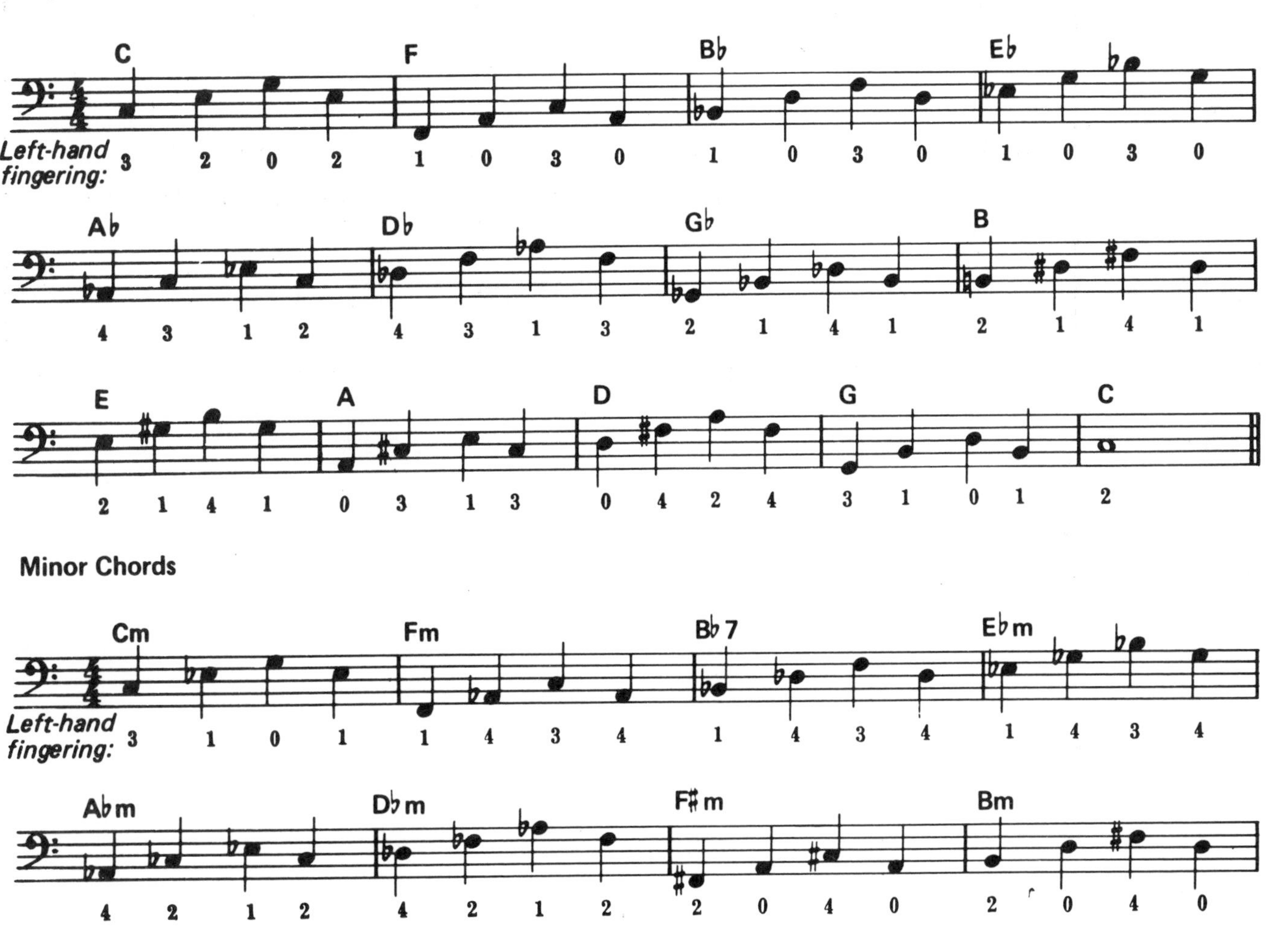

Augmented Chords

Diminished Chords

Diatonic Seventh Chords

Diatonic seventh chords differ from the chords that you have already learned in that they contain four notes instead of three. The "seventh" in the term *diatonic seventh* refers to the fact that the additional note is the seventh degree in a scale, and that the distance from the root of the chord to the top note is a seventh. For example, the notes of a C Major Seventh chord (CM7) are C, E, G, and B. The interval between C and B is a seventh.

Forming Diatonic Seventh Chords

Below is an F Major scale. Earlier we learned that by taking the first, third, and fifth notes of the major scale we could form a major chord, or *triad.* Adding the seventh note from the scale to this triad will form a major seventh chord.

Seventh chords can be built in any key and from any degree in the scale. Because only the natural, unaltered notes are used when constructing diatonic seventh chords, the type or quality of the chord that results from building on each separate note is different.

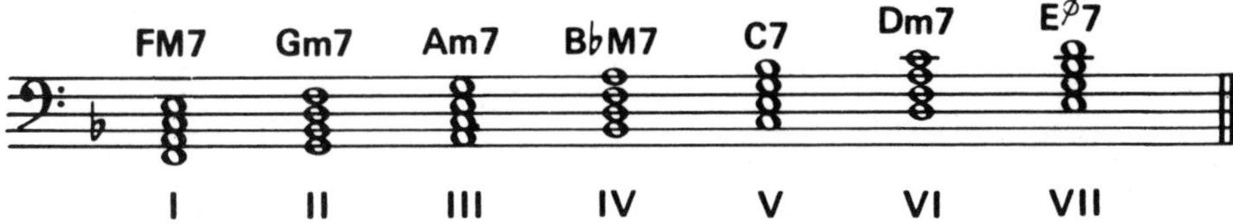

In the example above, we see all of the chords found in the F Major scale. The Roman numerals below each chord indicate the numbered position of the chords within the major scale.
The following rules and symbols apply to *all* chords in *all* major keys:

The I and IV chords are major sevenths.
(M7)

The II, III, and VI chords are minor sevenths.
(m7)

The V chord is a dominant seventh.
(7)

The VII chord is a half-diminished chord, sometimes called a minor seventh, flat-five.
(ø or m7 ♭5)

Playing the Seventh in a Bass Line

So far we have used only the root, third, and fifth of the chord in our exercises. Play through the examples below to hear how seventh chords fit into a bass line.

Major Seventh Chords

Dominant Seventh Chords

Minor Seventh Chords

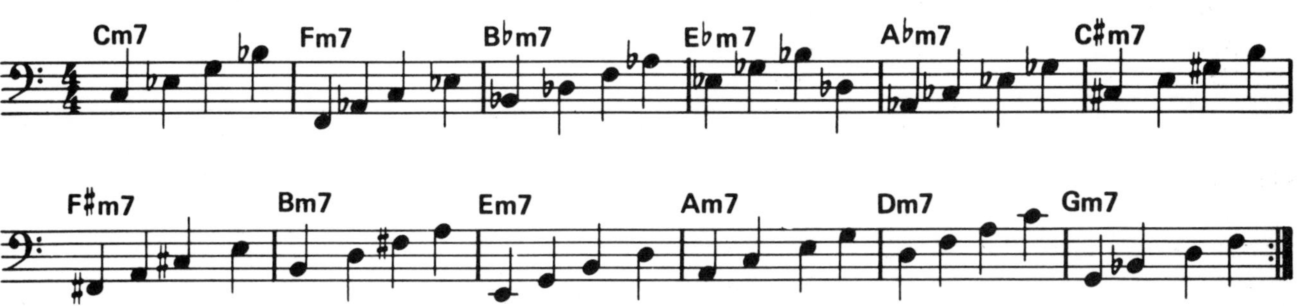

Half-Diminished or Minor Seventh, Flat-Five Chords

Diminished Seventh Chords

The diminished seventh chord does not occur naturally in the series of diatonic sevenths, and is constructed by using accidentals. It is often found in many popular and jazz compositions.

In the following exercises, all double-flats have been eliminated by using their enharmonic equivalents. For example, C°7 would normally contain the notes C, E♭, G♭ and B♭♭. Instead of the B♭♭, I have used the enharmonic equivalent A♮

Below are some examples of bass lines that use various sevenths. Try playing each example in different keys.

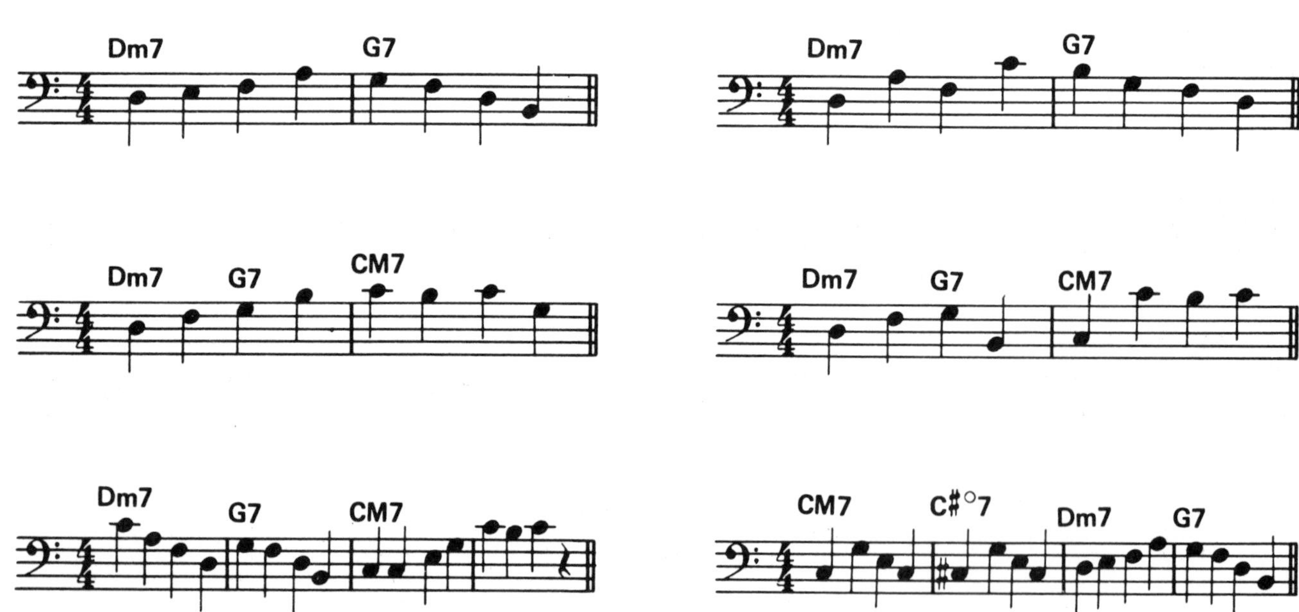

Progressions

A progression is a series of connected chords. Examining a large number of compositions shows that certain progressions occur again and again. It is important for you to become familiar with the most common progressions.

The II V I Progression

II V I is the most important progression and is the backbone of almost all jazz and popular compositions. Because the II (supertonic), V (dominant), and I (tonic) chords are so strongly related harmonically, they can be thought of as *primary chords.*

Primary chords are the chords that define the key. When a musician sees these chords, he should know immediately where the tonal center of the piece is, or whether a key change is pending.

Building a Bass Line in the II V I Progression

The first step in building a bass line is to begin with roots and fifths. The following exercise is based on the roots and fifths played through the II V I chords in every key.

In this next example based on the II V I progression, the bass line includes thirds.

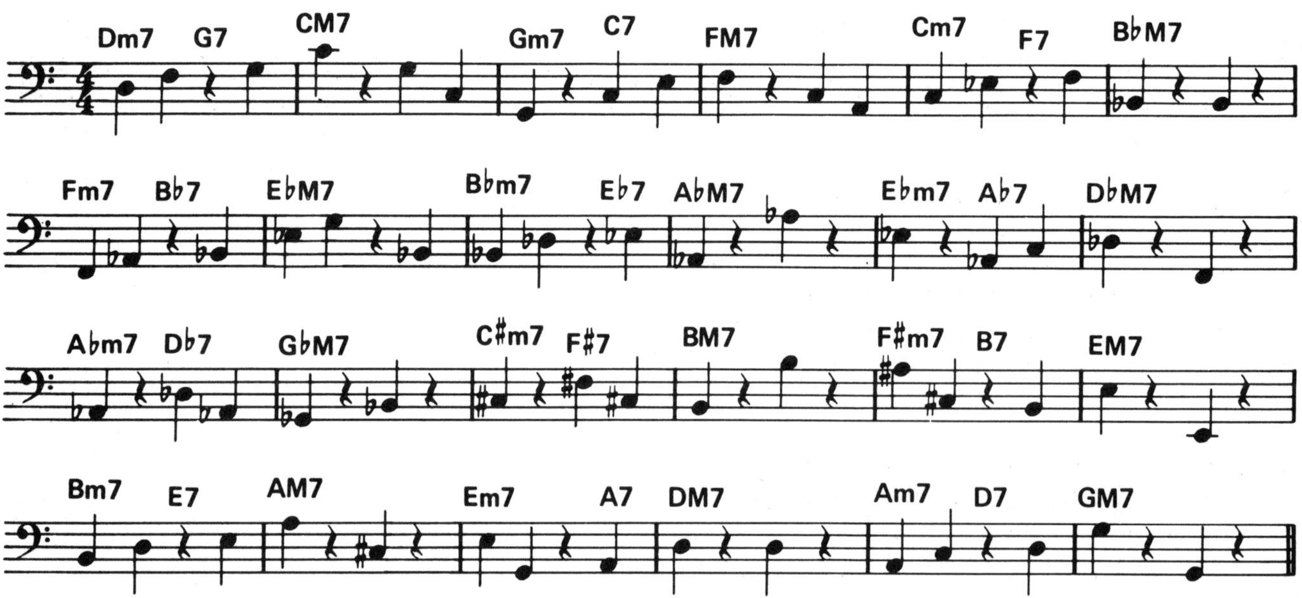

There are no rests in the next exercise; you'll be playing a note for every beat.

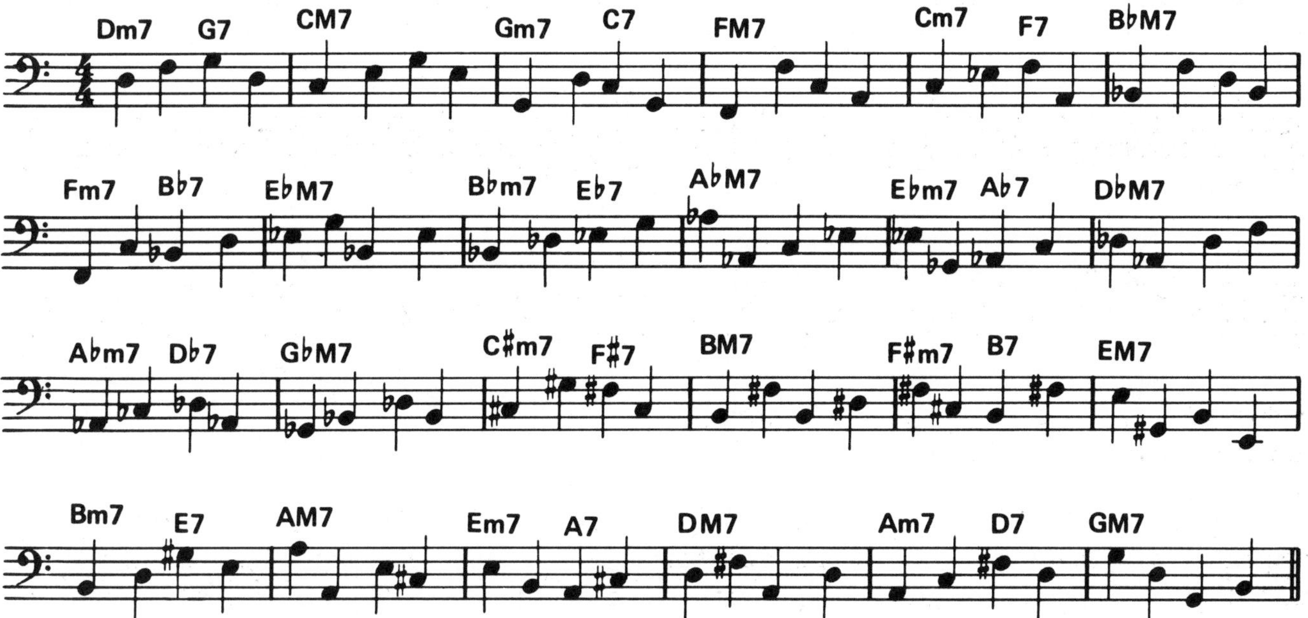

II V Progressions and Walking Bass Lines

Frequently a composition will contain several sequences of II V progressions before resolving to the I chord. The following exercises will give you a feel for this kind of progression in each key.

Notice that there are notes used that are not found in the original triad of the chord. These nonchord tones are called *passing tones.* In the next two exercises, they are one *whole step* up from the root of each chord. The use of passing tones in addition to chord tones when constructing a bass line is called a *walking bass.*

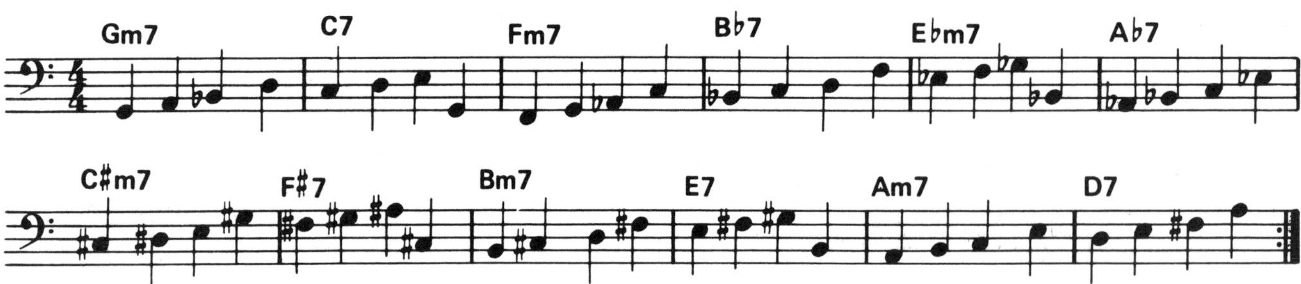

These next bass lines are similar to the ones above, except that the fifth of each chord has been flatted to create a smoother approach to the root of the following chords.

When the II and V chords are played in the same measure for two counts each, the chromatic (half step) approach may still be used.

In this next example we see the II chord approaching the V chord from a half step below and then the V chord moving to the II chord of the next key from a half step above.

The Circle of Fifths

The diagram below shows the circle of fifths. It is a way of arranging chords, or keys. Not only should it be memorized because it represents the key signatures in their natural order, but, since many popular compositions consist of chord progressions that move through the circle of fifths (V to I), the bass player should familiarize himself with the circle counterclockwise: in descending fourths.

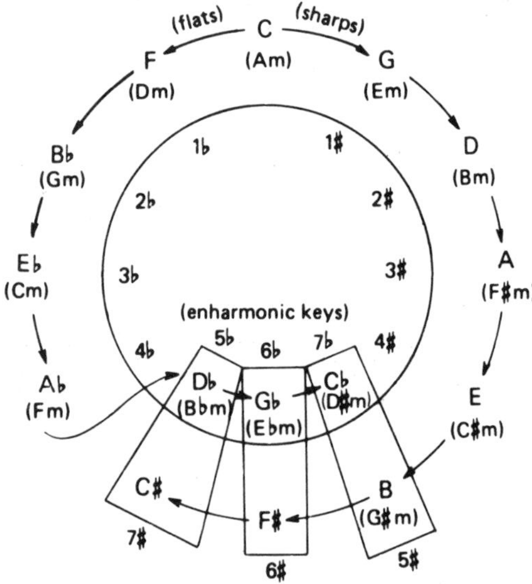

"All the Things You Are," "Satin Doll," and "I Got Rhythm" are all good examples of pieces where the bass player must play through the circle. In fact, because of the strong natural harmonic pull from the V chord to the I, most of the exercises that begin on page 37 are based on the circle of fifths.

The following exercise illustrates a bass line played through a series of V7 chords that move through the complete circle.

More II V I Progressions

The next two exercises are based on the II V I progression played through the circle of fifths. Notice that the roots of the chords progress around the circle until they repeat.

More Rhythm

A bass line that is harmonically interesting should be interesting rhythmically as well. So far all our lines have been based on quarter notes. By adding ties and dotted quarter notes combined with eighth notes, we can create a more exciting bass line.

Tied Notes

A curved line connecting two notes of the same pitch is called a *tie.* It indicates that the duration of the first note is increased by the time value of the second note.

Dotted Quarter Notes

A dot following one note increases that note's time value by *one-half* that of the original note. A dotted quarter note is equal to a quarter note tied to an eighth note.

This familiar melody uses both dotted quarter and dotted half notes.

Auld Lang Syne

Traditional

I IV V Blues Progressions

The blues, one of the most fundamental forms of jazz and popular music, is the subject of the next series of examples. The basic blues progression—I to IV to V—was used by the earliest bass players and is still used by blues and rock players today. Because of the simplicity of the constant repetition of I IV V, blues progressions are a good place to begin to learn how to create an interesting flowing bass line through rhythmic variation. Our first example showing the use of eighth notes and dotted quarter notes is typical of early rock/blues bass lines; only the root, third, and fifth are used.

This next example is in G Major. Notice that the sixth has been added.

In this next example the I chord is treated as a dominant seventh (F7), a common practice among many blues players. The II chord is placed before the F7 in measure 4 (Cm7 F7). The C7 chord, normally played in measure 9, is moved over one measure and its II chord (Gm7) used to prepare the C7. In measure 8, a Dm7 (VI) chord is used between the I (F7) and the II (Gm7), again common practice. In measures 11 and 12, is a progression I VI II V (F7 Dm7 Gm7 C7), known as the *turnaround* and used when returning to measure 1.

The next blues bass line is a bit more modern than the one above. In measure 7, the III chord (Bm7) is used as a substitute for the I chord (GM7). Turnaround chords are again used in measures 11 and 12, and the chromatic movement in measures 1 and 2 makes the whole line smoother.

Sixteenth Notes

Quarter notes and eighth notes can be subdivided into *sixteenth notes.* Two sixteenth notes equal one eighth note, four sixteenth notes equal a quarter note. They can be written by using either a double flag (for single sixteenth notes) or a double beam (for two or more sixteenth notes).

In the two exercises below, the eighth notes are played on the beat, the sixteenth notes off the beat. We'll use the vowel sound "a" (pronounced *uh*) in addition to "and" to represent the extra beat.

In the following exercises the sixteenth notes are played on the beat, the eighth notes off the beat.

Playing two sixteenth notes on the beat and two sixteenth notes off the beat results in the following rhythm.

In these next exercises, be sure to hold each quarter note for its full value.

This study is based on major chords.

This is the same study as the one above, but with sixteenth notes tied to eighth notes.

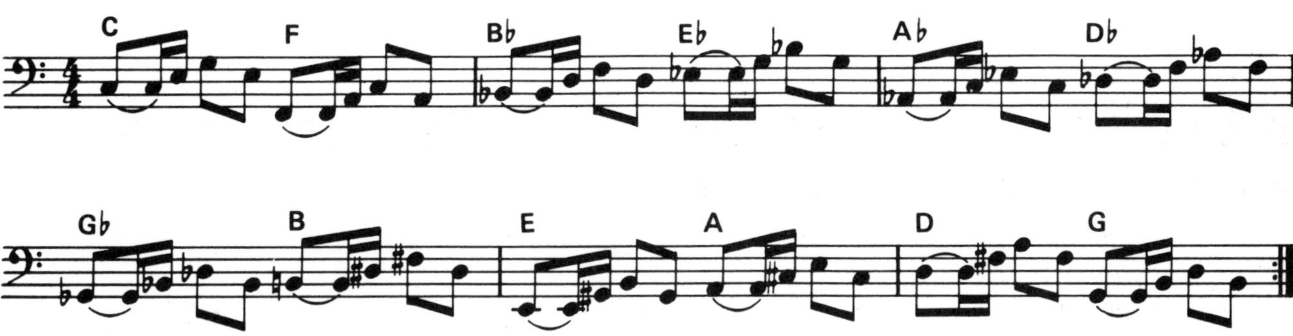

Dotted Eighth Notes

The following study is the same as the one you just played except that the dotted eighth note has replaced the eighth note tied to the sixteenth note.

In the following exercise, be sure to feel the difference between the even eighth notes and the dotted eighth notes followed by the sixteenth notes.

The I VI II V Progression

Another standard progression is I VI II V, which is found in many familiar tunes, such as "Blue Moon," "These Foolish Things," "Heart and Soul," and "Ringo's Theme (This Boy)."

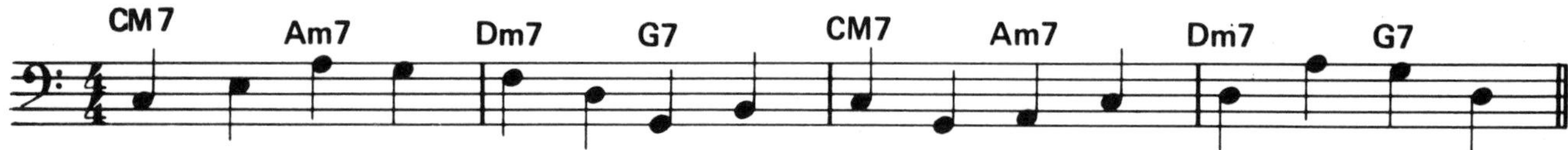

Variations on I VI II V

Here are several variations of the I VI II V progression. It's important to realize that hundreds of possible lines exist for any progression. At this point you should be trying to invent your own bass lines for the progressions given so far.
Notice the chromatic approach to the chord root, and keep the sixteenth notes short.

Watch out for the even eighth notes.

Notice the sequence of notes leading from V back to I.

This is similar to the above except for the descending notes into chord roots.

Watch the tied notes. Measures 3 and 4 look different from the first two measures but are played exactly the same. The eighth-note-quarter-note-eighth-note figure is a form of *syncopation.*

This example combines dotted quarter notes with a syncopated figure. Notice the sequence of notes that takes V back to I.

Triplets

Three eighth notes beamed together with a *3* above constitute an eighth-note *triplet.* The three notes of the triplet are played in the same time as one quarter note.

The first note of each triplet must be played on the beat. Play all three notes evenly so that the last note of the triplet flows smoothly into the following beat.

The following study is based on dominant seventh chords in the circle of fifths. Play the triplets smoothly and evenly.

Extending the Fingerboard

Now that you are familiar with the notes on the first four frets of each string, we are going to learn the notes on each string up to the twelfth fret.

Fourth String

Moveable Scales

A moveable scale is a scale that does not contain any open-string notes. As a result, it can be played anywhere on the neck and will retain the same pitch relationships. The diagram below illustrates the fingering for the major scale.

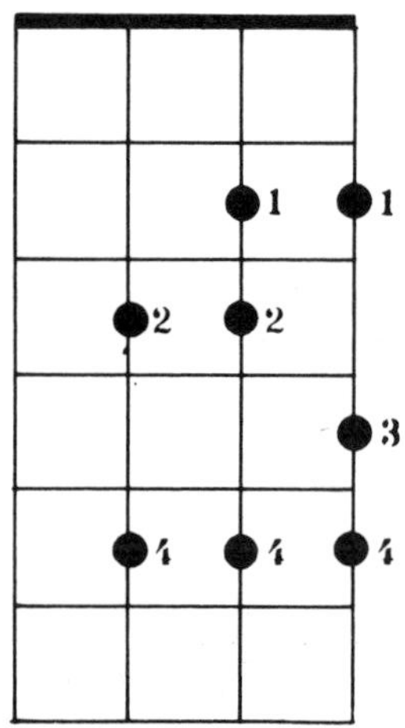

All of the following major scales are to be played using the fingering given above.

C Scale 3rd Fret, 3rd String

G Scale, 3rd Fret, 4th String

D♭ Scale, 4th Fret, 3rd String
2 4 1 2 4 1 3 4 3 1 4 2 1 4 2
A♭ Scale, 4th Fret, 4th String
2 4 1 2 4 1 3 4 3 1 4 2 1 4 2
D Scale, 5th Fret, 3rd String
2 4 1 2 4 1 3 4 3 1 4 2 1 4 2
A Scale, 5th Fret, 4th String
2 4 1 2 4 1 3 4 3 1 4 2 1 4 2
E♭ Scale, 6th Fret, 3rd String
2 4 1 2 4 1 3 4 3 1 4 2 1 4 2
B♭ Scale, 6th Fret, 4th String
2 4 1 2 4 1 3 4 3 1 4 2 1 4 2
E Scale, 7th Fret, 3rd String
2 4 1 2 4 1 3 4 3 1 4 2 1 4 2

B Scale, 7th Fret, 4th String

F Scale, 8th Fret, 3rd String

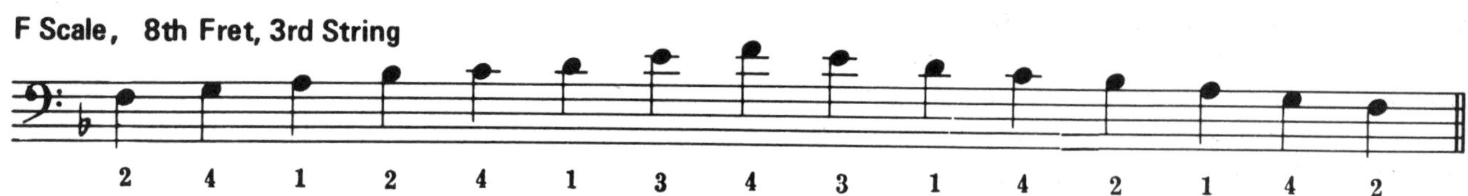

C Scale, 8th Fret, 4th String

Technique Builders

The following patterns written in the key of C should be practiced at different frets on the neck. Move systematically up the neck by half steps to make sure that you've played the exercise in all possible keys.

Position Playing

Position playing means playing anywhere on the fingerboard without using open strings. A position occupies four frets plus a stretch up or down of one fret. A position is named by the fret where your first finger is located. For example, second position means that your first finger plays all the notes at the second fret, your second finger plays all the notes at the third fret, and so forth. The following pieces should be played in the second position. Remember, *no open strings.*

Etude

Minuet

Johann Sebastian Bach
1685-1750

Moveable Chords

Like scales, chords can be played using no open strings and moved all over the fingerboard. The moveable chords given below are all played with the second finger on the fourth string.

G

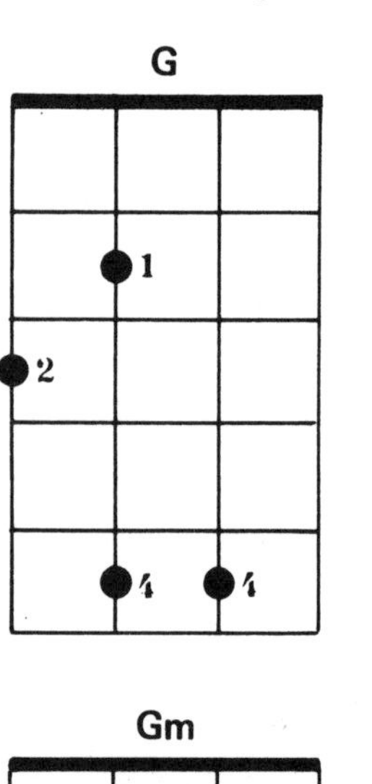

GM7

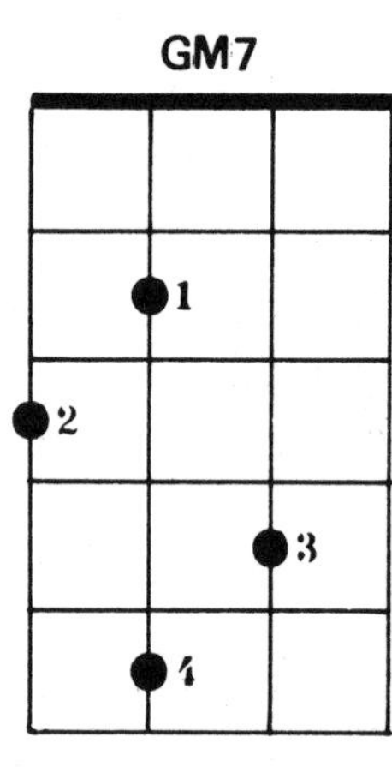

G7

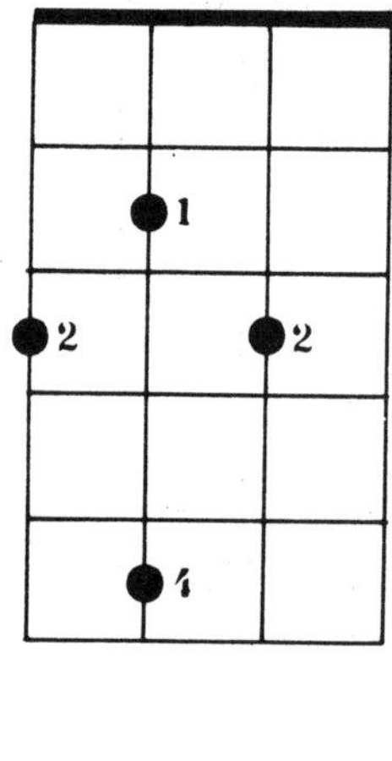

G6

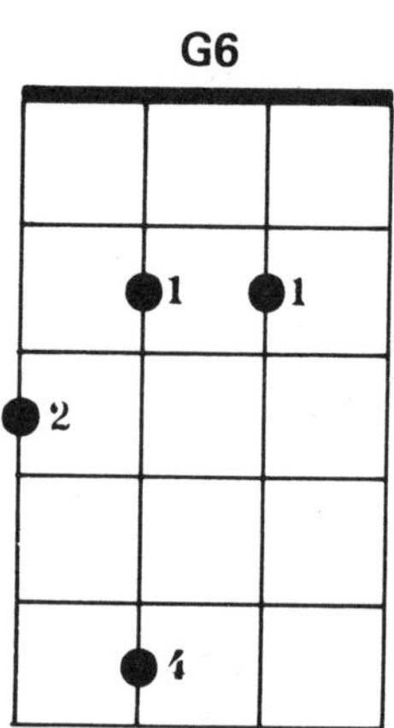

Gm

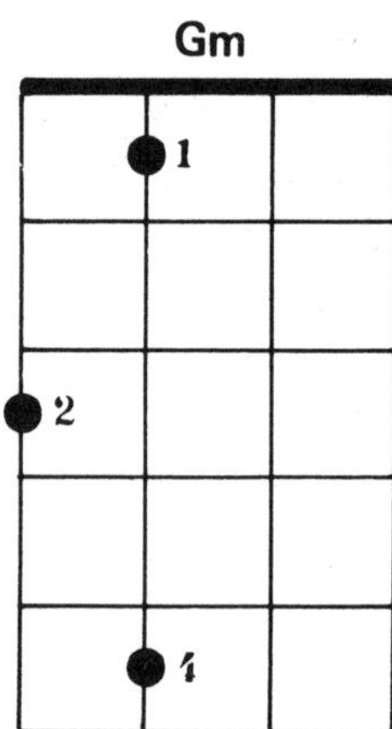

Gm7

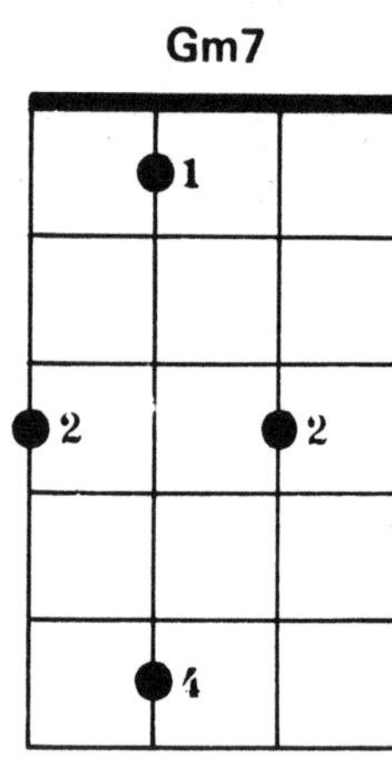

The G6 chord shown above is often used as a substitute for the I chord.

G
GM7
G7
G6
Gm
Gm7
2 1 4 4
2 1 4 3
2 1 4 2
2 1 4 1
2 1 4
2 1 4 2

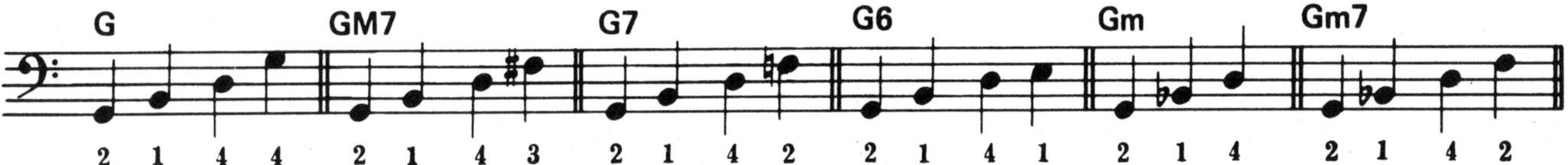

Here are chords that start with the second finger but are played starting on the third string.

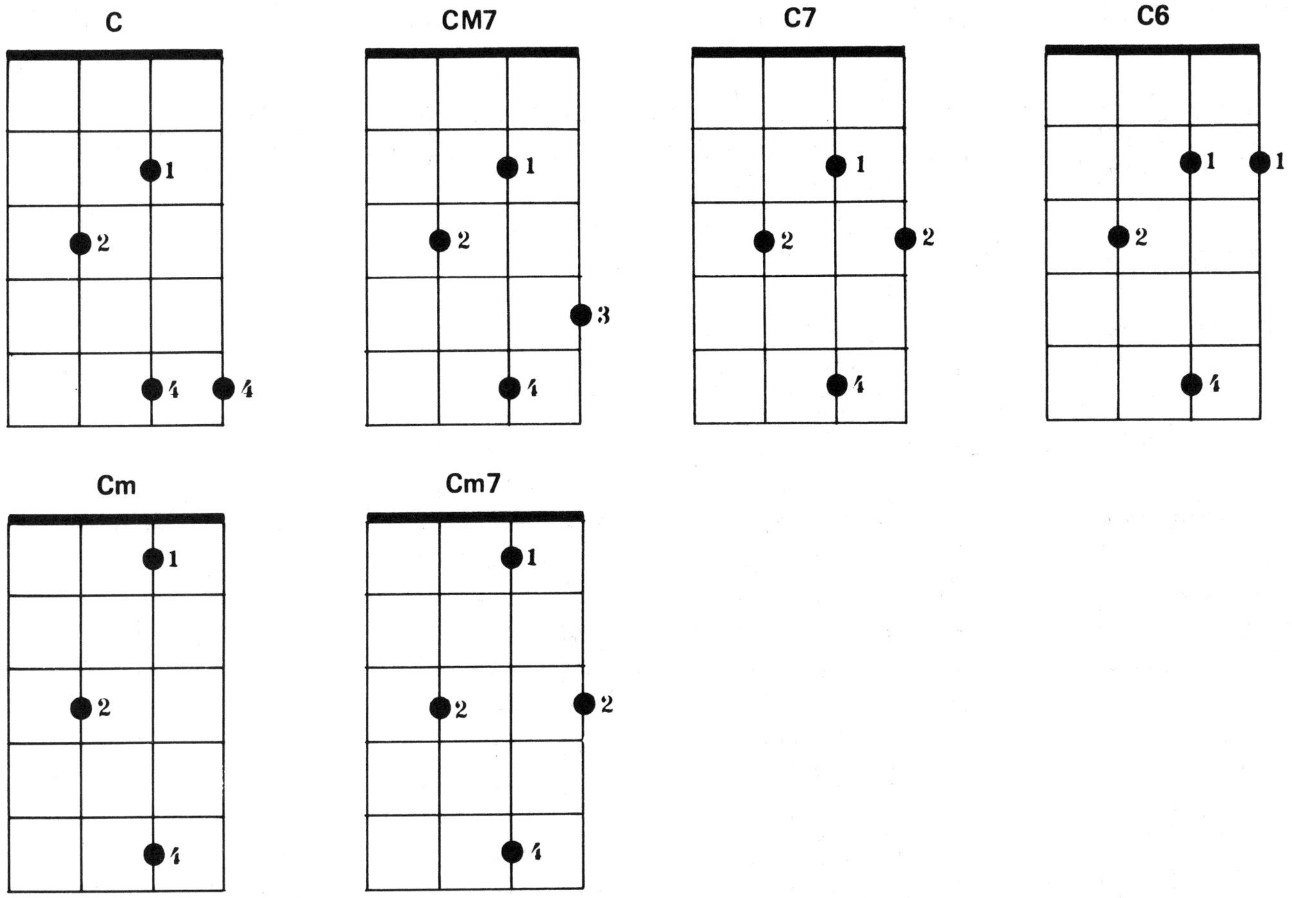
C
CM7
C7
C6
Cm
Cm7

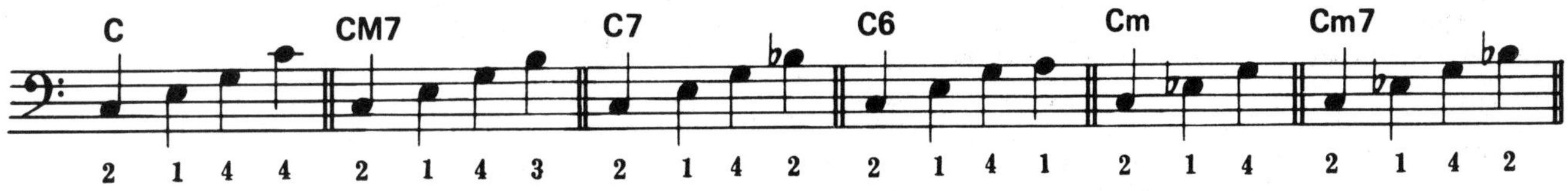
C
CM7
C7
C6
Cm
Cm7
2 1 4 4
2 1 4 3
2 1 4 2
2 1 4 1
2 1 4
2 1 4 2

Moveable Chords Played through the Circle of Fifths

Starting at the eighth fret on the fourth string, play the following exercise based on major chords played through the circle.

Continue the following exercises through the circle of fifths.

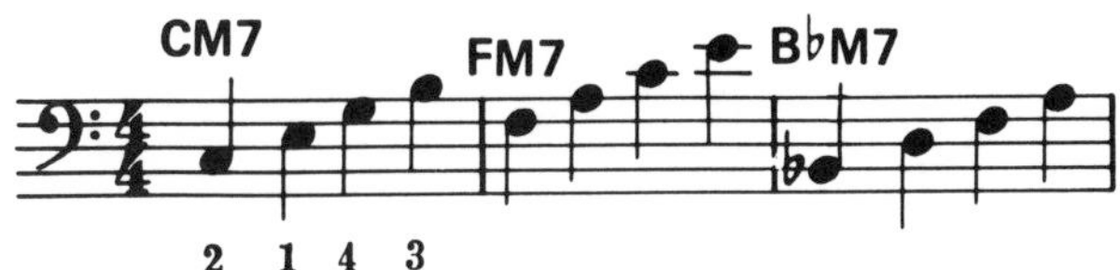

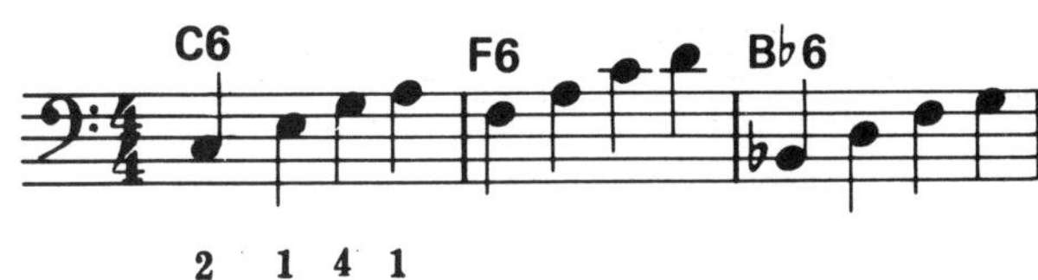

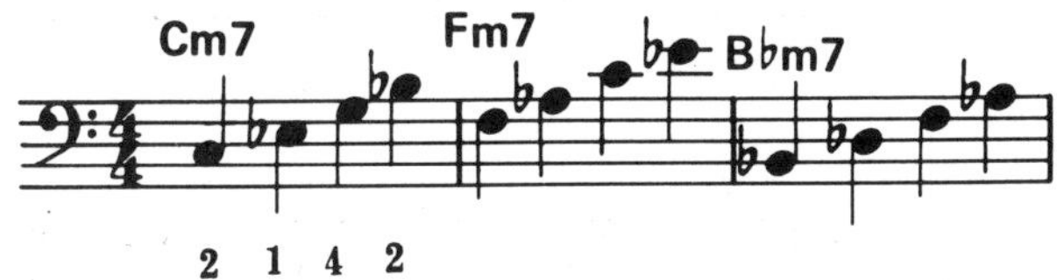

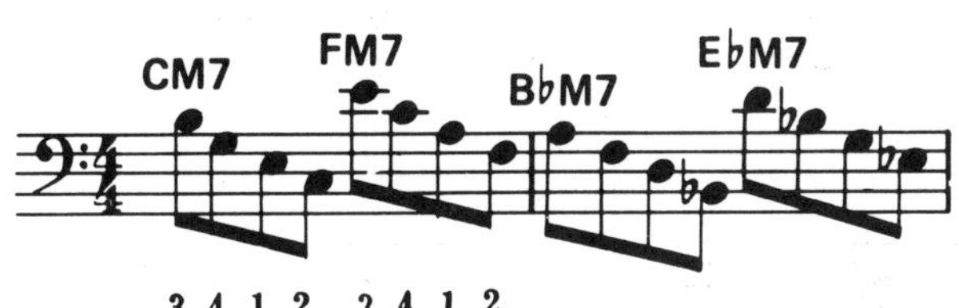

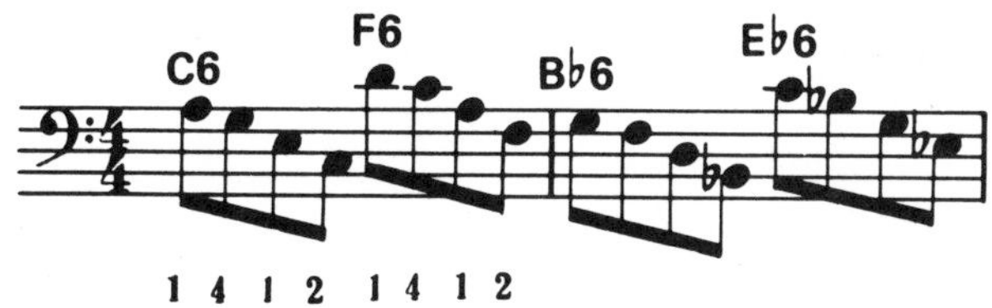

Moveable Bass Patterns

The advantage in knowing how to play moveable scales and chords is that you can now work out bass patterns that may be played anywhere on the fingerboard.
Below are several patterns based on the C Major chord. Memorize each pattern, then play it through the circle of fifths.

Pattern 1
Notice the use of octaves, C to C. An alternate fingering (1) is given for the lower C. This pattern may be played either from the third string, third fret or from the fourth string, eighth fret. Since the pattern uses only the root, third, and fifth, it may be used for either a C chord or a C7.

Pattern 2

This typical early blues patten combines the sixth and the dominant seventh.

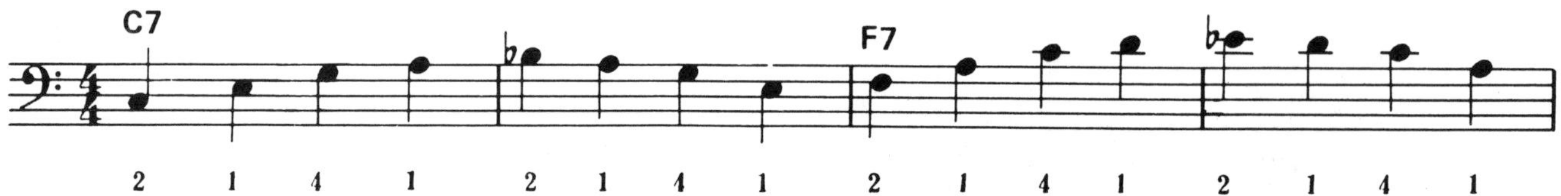

Pattern 3

Count the syncopation carefully on the first two beats and watch the tied note going into the third beat.

Pattern 4

In this simple early rock pattern be sure to hold the dotted quarter note for the full count.

Pattern 5

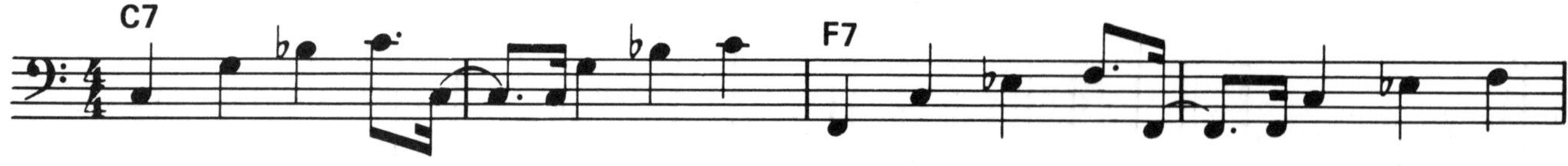

Octave Studies

Octave studies are an essential part of a bass player's development. The following studies are designed to help develop this technique.

These octave studies move through the circle of fifths.

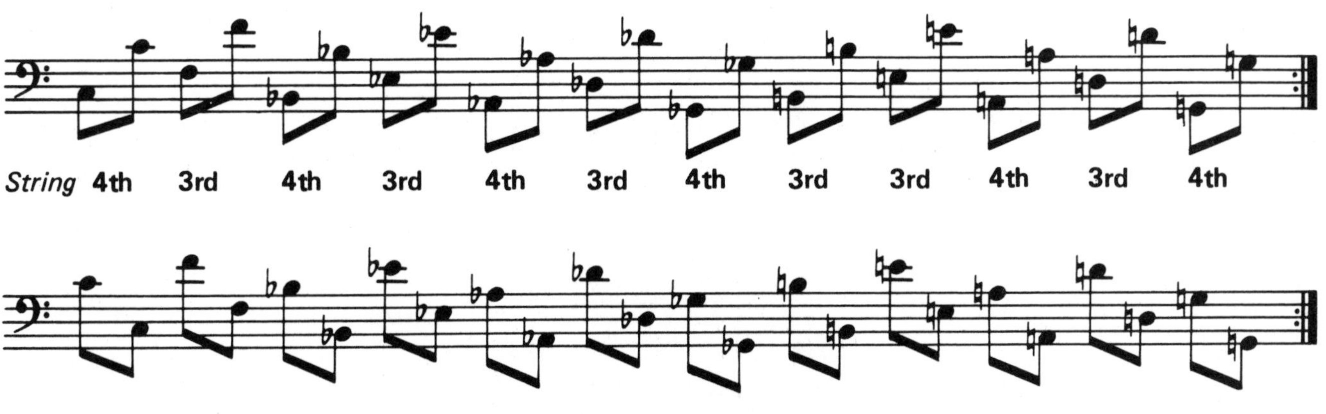

Octave Studies with Fifths

The following studies are based on roots, fifths, and octaves, all important ingredients in so many bass lines. After playing both studies as written try to play them through the circle.

Octave Studies with Sevenths

Continue these next two exercises up on the fingerboard.

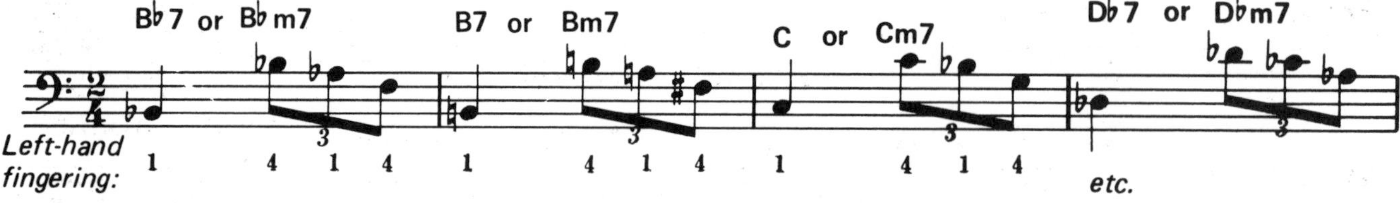

Continue this next exercise through the circle of fifths.

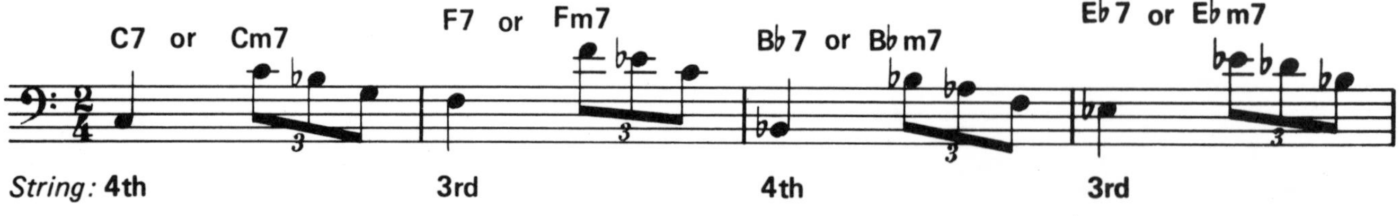

Octave Studies in Sixteenth Notes

Play the following study through the circle.

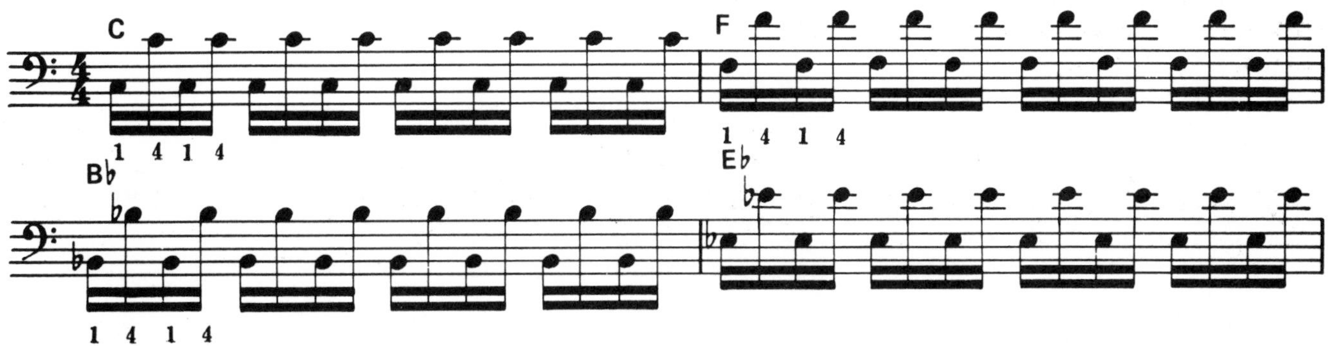

In this next study, notice how each chord moves to the next through the third. Complete the study through the rest of the circle.

Do the same for this next study using minor chords.

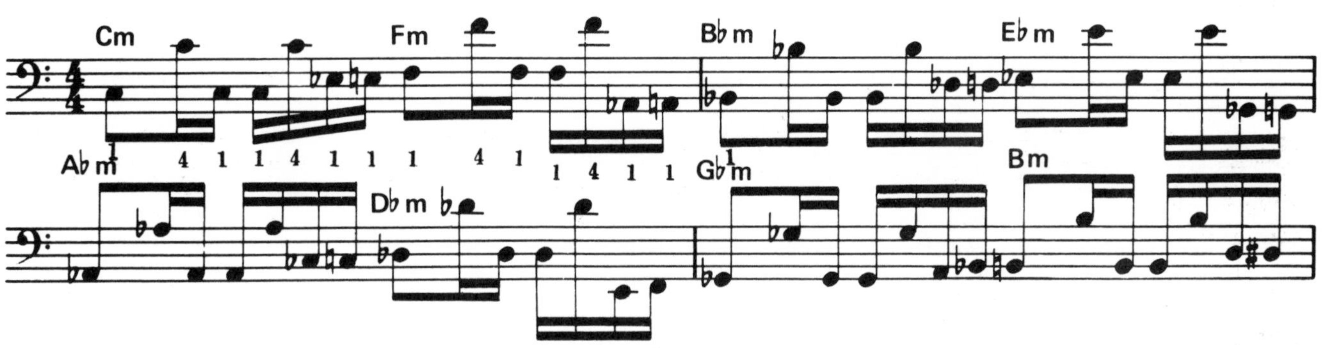

Modal Playing

Modes are scales with an arrangement of whole and half steps different from that of a major scale. Below are examples of all the modes that can be built from a C Major scale.

Ionian (or Major) Mode

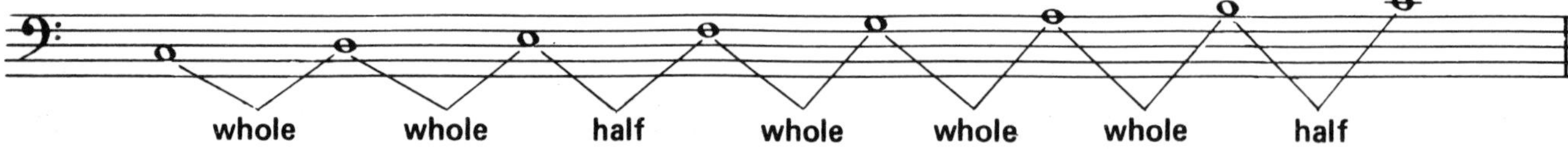

Dorian Mode

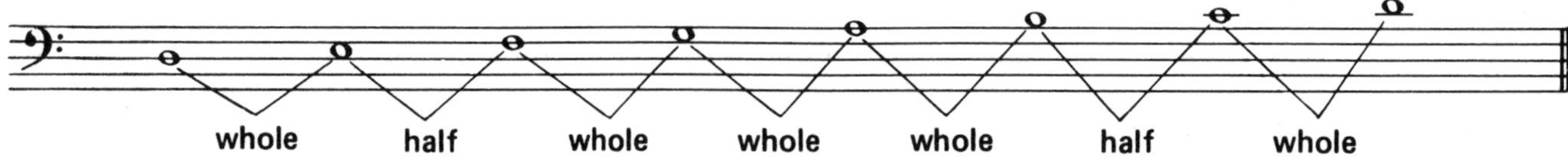

Phrygian Mode

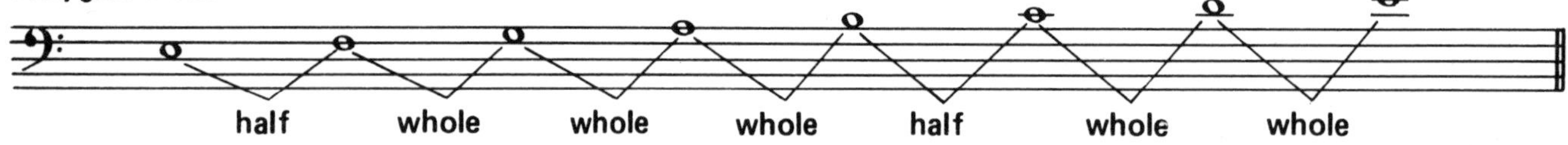

Lydian Mode

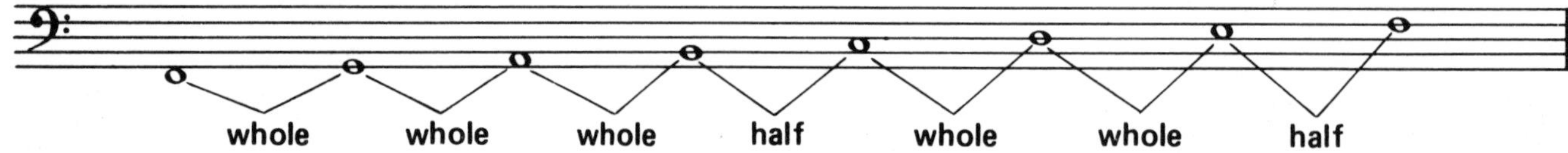

Mixolydian Mode

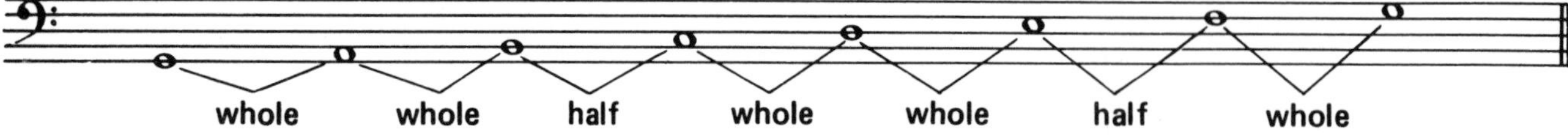

Aeolian (or Natural Minor) Mode

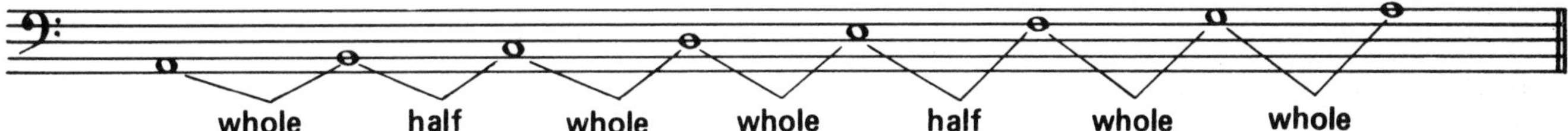

Locrian Mode

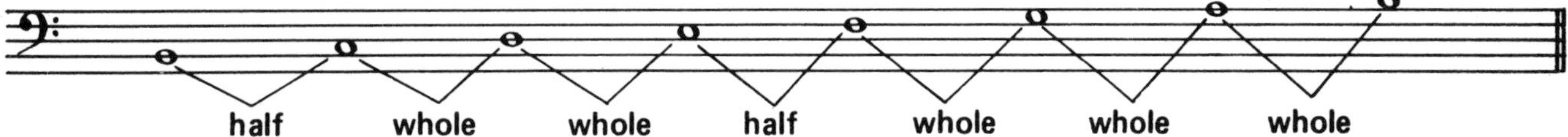

Although the modes given above occur naturally and without accidentals in the C Major scale, the name of each mode refers to the sound of the scale or piece (tonality) rather than to the note of the C Major scale on which it starts. For example, it is not uncommon to see a G Phrygian or a B♭ Mixolydian, or a C Dorian mode.

In 1959 Miles Davis released his album *Kind of Blue.* On it was "So What," a tune written in the Dorian mode that started a whole new interest in writing pieces based on modes rather than on chords. Modal compositions usually use just one mode, but the use of several in one composition is not unknown.

Below are several examples of fingerings for the C Dorian scale.

Sustaining musical interest when playing a song that contains only one or two chords can be quite a challenge. The following is one possibility when faced with a song using the C Dorian mode for sixteen measures.

Remember that the Dorian mode may be used for any unaltered minor chord such as a minor seventh, minor ninth, or minor eleventh.

Chromatic Scales

Chromatic scales progress in half steps. It is essential to learn to play chromatic patterns in every position. The following chromatic studies are based on playing across the strings (using open strings) and vertically (up and down on the same string).

The following studies are played along the same string. Of the two fingerings given, use the one that is most comfortable for your hand. Make sure that the shift from the fourth finger to the first finger is smooth, with no break in the rhythm. Play slowly.

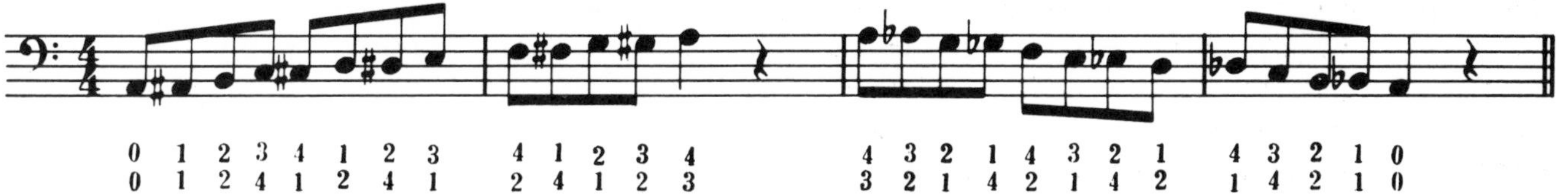

Chromatics in Bass Lines

A commonly used chromatic run is from the third of a chord to the fifth. Play the examples below through the circle of fifths.

This is the same exercise by using minor chords.

More Moveable Scales

Here is another moveable fingering for the major scale. It begins with the first finger. Scales may be played starting on the fourth string or the third string while keeping the same fingering.

F Scale (4th string)

B♭ Scale (3rd string)

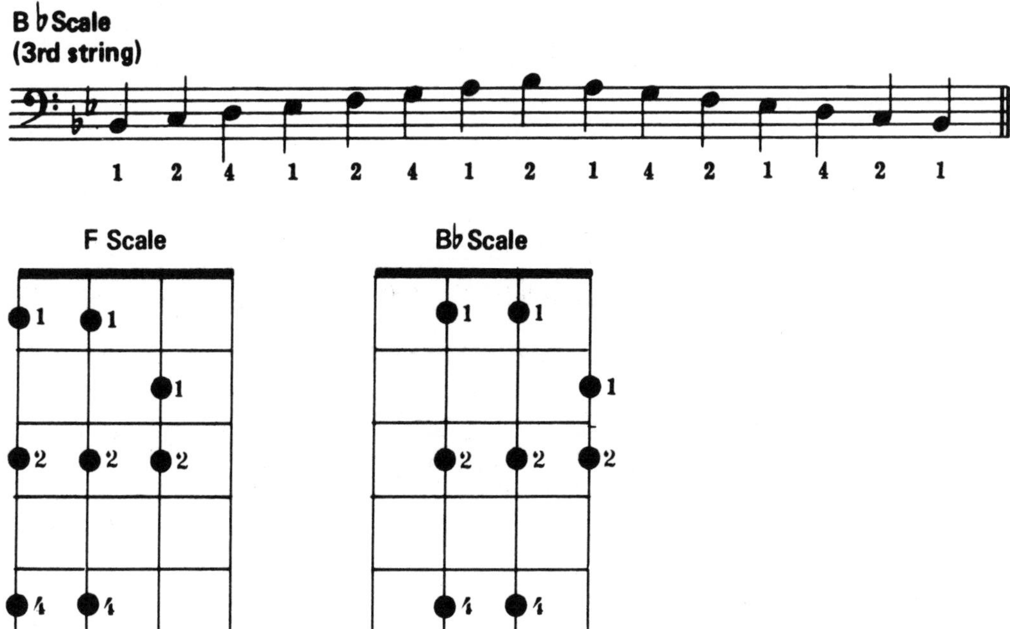

Try playing the scales through the circle starting from C.

Technique Builders

The following exercises will help you develop facility with the new scale fingering. Play each exercise through the circle starting with the key of F. Also try starting each exercise in the key of C.

More Moveable Chords

Below are various moveable chords that may be played starting with the first finger on the fourth string.

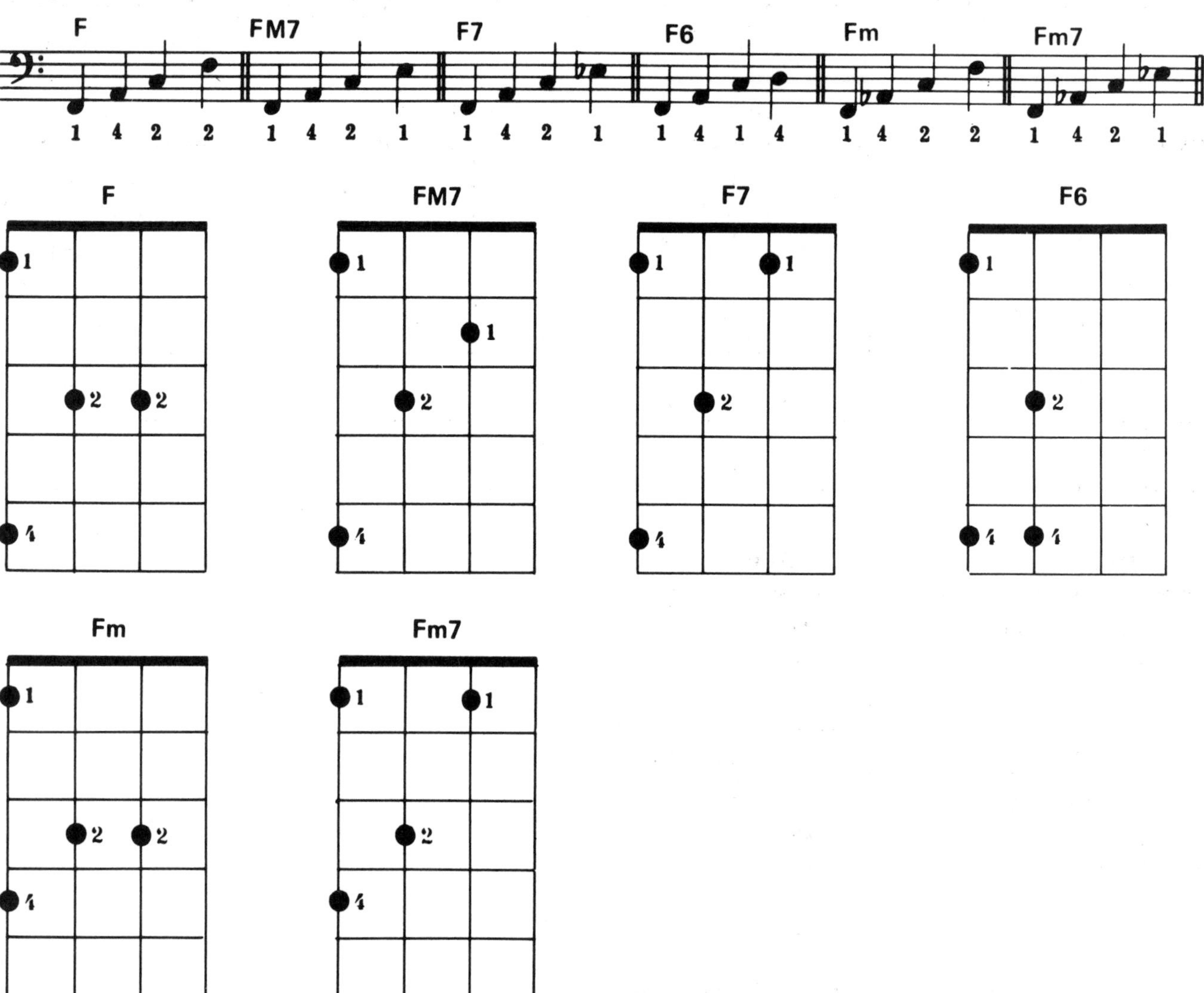

Here are more moveable chords, starting with the first finger on the third string.

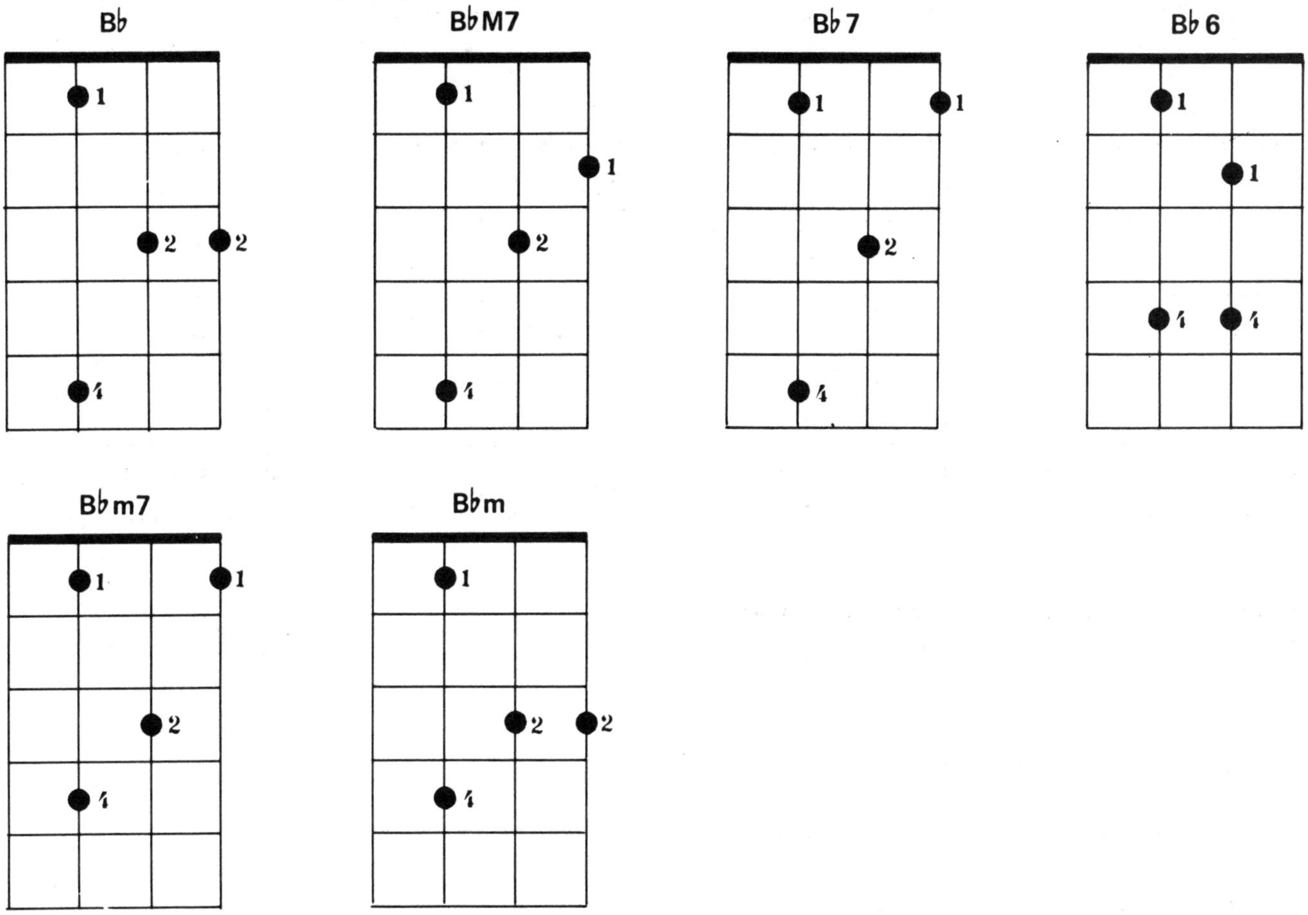

Bb — 1 4 2 2
BbM7 — 1 4 2 1
Bb7 — 1 4 2 1
Bb6 — 1 4 1 4
Bbm — 1 4 2 2
Bbm7 — 1 4 2 1

Bb

BbM7

Bb7

Bb6

Bbm7

Bbm

Play each of the above chord types through the circle by combining chords that begin with the second finger with chords that begin with the first finger.

Vamps

Besides being able to create smooth, flowing bass lines you should be able to create interesting one- or two-measure *vamps.* A vamp is a rhythmic figure that is repeated over and over either as an introduction or as a filler between two different sections of music.

Below are several examples of one- and two-measure vamps based on a C7 chord. The examples show the unlimited rhythmic choices that are available based on just the notes of the chord. The greater the rhythmic variety, the greater the interest to the soloist and the listener.

One-Measure Vamps

Two-Measure Vamps

3/4 Time Signature

Bass players are required to play music written with all kinds of time signatures. In recent years a number of jazz waltzes have been composed, for example, "Waltz for Debby," by Bill Evans, "Three Flowers," by McCoy Tyner, and "Little Waltz" by Ron Carter. Below are several examples of bass lines played in $\frac{3}{4}$.

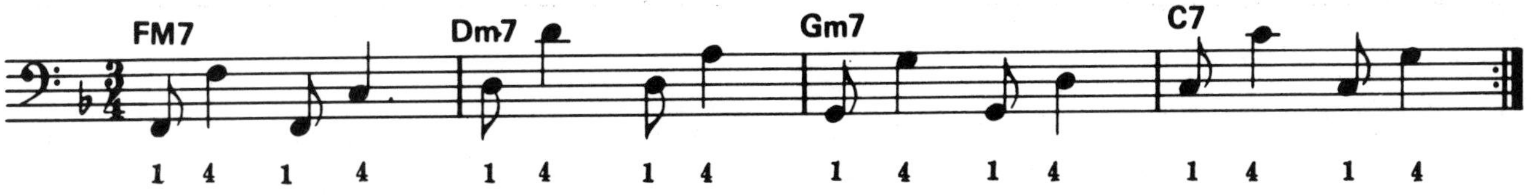

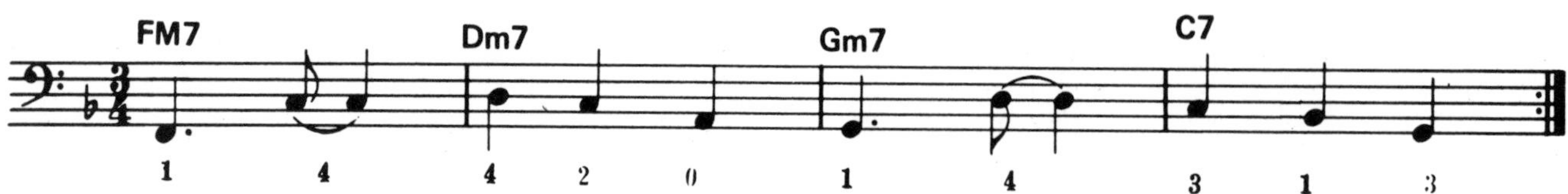

6/8 Time Signature

Although $\frac{6}{8}$ time is not commonly found in jazz, more composers are now beginning to use it. Chick Corea, for example, has written several pieces in $\frac{6}{8}$, including "Litha" and "La Fiesta."

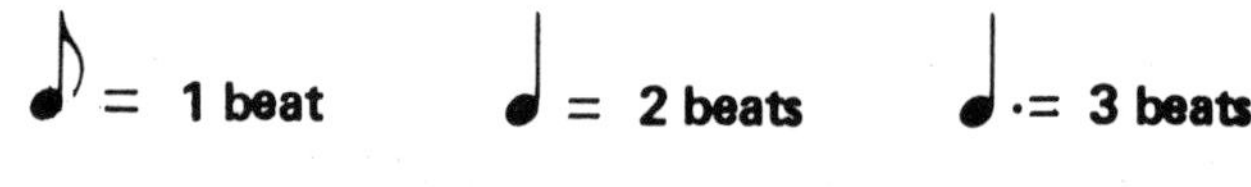

By looking at the example above, you can see that in $\frac{6}{8}$, an eighth note gets one beat. This is true of all time signatures that have an eight on the bottom, such as $\frac{3}{8}$, $\frac{9}{8}$, and $\frac{12}{8}$. The dotted quarter note in $\frac{6}{8}$ is important as it equals half a measure. There will be times when it is easiest to think of a measure of $\frac{6}{8}$ as two groups of three.

Jonathan's Jig

Stir Fry
CM7
Am7
A♭7
G7
CM7
Am7
A♭7
G7
CM7
Am7
A♭7
G7
CM7
A7
A♭7
G7
Cm7
A7
A♭7
G7
CM7
A7
A♭7
G7
C